Milwaukee Brewers 2021

A Baseball Companion

Edited by Steven Goldman and Bret Sayre

Baseball Prospectus

Craig Brown, Associate Editor
Robert Au, Harry Pavlidis and Amy Pircher, Statistics Editors

Copyright © 2021 by DIY Baseball, LLC.
All rights reserved

This book or any part thereof may not be reproduced or transmitted in any form or by any means, electronic or mechanical, including photocopying, recording, or by any information storage and retrieval system, without permission in writing from the publisher.

Limit of Liability/Disclaimer of Warranty: While the publisher and the author have used their best efforts in preparing this book, they make no representations or warranties with respect to the accuracy or completeness of the contents of this book and specifically disclaim any implied warranties of merchantability or fitness for a particular purpose. No warranty may be created or extended by sales representatives or written sales materials. The advice and strategies contained herein may not be suitable for your situation. You should consult with a professional where appropriate. Neither the publisher nor the author shall be liable for any loss of profit or any other commercial damages, including but not limited to special, incidental, consequential, or other damages.

Library of Congress Cataloging-in-Publication Data:
paperback
ISBN-13: 978-1-950716-55-5

Project Credits
Cover Design: Ginny Searle
Interior Design and Production: Amy Pircher, Robert Au
Layout: Amy Pircher, Robert Au

Baseball icon courtesy of Uberux, from https://www.shareicon.net/author/uberux

Ballpark diagram courtesy of Lou Spirito/THIRTY81 Project, https://thirty81project.com/

Manufactured in the United States of America
10 9 8 7 6 5 4 3 2 1

Table of Contents

Statistical Introduction v

Part 1: Team Analysis

Performance Graphs 3
2020 Team Performance 4
2021 Team Projections 5
Team Personnel 6
Miller Park Stats 7
Brewers Team Analysis 9

Part 2: Player Analysis

Brewers Player Analysis 16
Brewers Prospects 91

Part 3: Featured Articles

Brewers All-Time Top 10 Players 103
    by Matthew Trueblood

A Taxonomy of 2020 Abnormalities 109
    by Rob Mains

Tranches of WAR 115
    by Russell A. Carleton

Secondhand Sport 121
    by Patrick Dubuque

Steve Dalkowski Dreaming 125
    by Steven Goldman

A Reward For A Functioning Society 129
    by Cory Frontin and Craig Goldstein

Index of Names 133

Statistical Introduction

Sports are, fundamentally, a blend of athletic endeavor and storytelling. Baseball, like any other sport, tells its stories in so many ways: in the arc of a game from the stands or a season from the box scores, in photos, or even in numbers. At Baseball Prospectus, we understand that statistics don't replace observation or any of baseball's stories, but complement everything else that makes the game so much fun.

What stats help us with is with patterns and precision, variance and value. This book can help you learn things you may not see from watching a game or hundred, whether it's the path of a career over time or the breadth of the entire MLB. We'd also never ask you to choose between our numbers and the experience of viewing a game from the cheap seats or the comfort of your home; our publication combines running the numbers with observations and wisdom from some of the brightest minds we can find. But if you *do* want to learn more about the numbers beyond what's on the backs of player jerseys, let us help explain.

Offense

We've revised our methodology for determining batting value. Long-time readers of the book will notice that we've retired True Average in favor of a new metric: Deserved Runs Created Plus (DRC+). Developed by Jonathan Judge and our stats team, this statistic measures everything a player does at the plate–reaching base, hitting for power, making outs, and moving runners over–and puts it on a scale where 100 equals league-average performance. A DRC+ of 150 is terrific, a DRC+ of 100 is average and a DRC+ of 75 means you better be an excellent defender.

DRC+ also does a better job than any of our previous metrics in taking contextual factors into account. The model adjusts for how the park affects performance, but also for things like the talent of the opposing pitcher, value of different types of batted-ball events, league, temperature and other factors. It's able to describe a player's expected offensive contribution than any other statistic we've found over the years, and also does a better job of predicting future performance as well.

The other aspect of run-scoring is baserunning, which we quantify using Baserunning Runs. BRR not only records the value of stolen bases (or getting caught in the act), but also accounts for all the stuff that doesn't show up on the back of a baseball card: a runner's ability to go first to third on a single, or advance on a fly ball.

Defense

Where offensive value is *relatively* easy to identify and understand, defensive value is ... not. Over the past dozen years, the sabermetric community has focused mostly on stats based on zone data: a real-live human person records the type of batted ball and estimated landing location, and models are created that give expected outs. From there, you can compare fielders' actual outs to those expected ones. Simple, right?

Unfortunately, zone data has two major issues. First, zone data is recorded by commercial data providers who keep the raw data private unless you pay for it. (All the statistics we build in this book and on our website use public data as inputs.) That hurts our ability to test assumptions or duplicate results. Second, over the years it has become apparent that there's quite a bit of "noise" in zone-based fielding analysis. Sometimes the conclusions drawn from zone data don't hold up to scrutiny, and sometimes the different data provided by different providers don't look anything alike, giving wildly different results. Sometimes the hard-working professional stringers or scorers might unknowingly inflict unconscious bias into the mix: for example good fielders will often be credited with more expected outs despite the data, and ballparks with high press boxes tend to score more line drives than ones with a lower press box.

Enter our Fielding Runs Above Average (FRAA). For most positions, FRAA is built from play-by-play data, which allows us to avoid the subjectivity found in many other fielding metrics. The idea is this: count how many fielding plays are made by a given player and compare that to expected plays for an average fielder at their position (based on pitcher ground ball tendencies and batter handedness). Then we adjust for park and base-out situations.

When it comes to catchers, our methodology is a little different thanks to the laundry list of responsibilities they're tasked with beyond just, well, catching and throwing the ball. By now you've probably heard about "framing" or the art of making umpires more likely to call balls outside the strike zone for strikes. To put this into one tidy number, we incorporate pitch tracking data (for the years it exists) and adjust for important factors like pitcher, umpire, batter and home-field advantage using a mixed-model approach. This grants us a number for how many strikes the catcher is personally adding to (or subtracting from) his pitchers' performance ... which we then convert to runs added or lost using linear weights.

Framing is one of the biggest parts of determining catcher value, but we also take into account blocking balls from going past, whether a scorer deems it a passed ball or a wild pitch. We use a similar approach—one that really benefits from the pitch tracking data that tells us what ends up in the dirt and what doesn't. We also include a catcher's ability to prevent stolen bases and how well they field balls in play, and *finally* we come up with our FRAA for catchers.

Pitching

Both pitching and fielding make up the half of baseball that isn't run scoring: run prevention. Separating pitching from fielding is a tough task, and most recent pitching analysis has branched off from Voros McCracken's famous (and controversial) statement, "There is little if any difference among major-league pitchers in their ability to prevent hits on balls hit in the field of play." The research of the analytic community has validated this to some extent, and there are a host of "defense-independent" pitching measures that have been developed to try and extract the effect of the defense behind a hurler from the pitcher's work.

Our solution to this quandary is Deserved Run Average (DRA), our core pitching metric. DRA seeks to evaluate a pitcher's performance, much like earned run average (ERA), the tried-and-true pitching stat you've seen on every baseball broadcast or box score from the past century, but it's very different. To start, DRA takes an event-by-event look at what the pitchers does, and adjusts the value of that event based on different environmental factors like park, batter, catcher, umpire, base-out situation, run differential, inning, defense, home field advantage, pitcher role and temperature. That mixed model gives us a pitcher's expected contribution, similar to what we do for our DRC+ model for hitters and FRAA model for catchers. (Oh, and we also consider the pitcher's effect on basestealing and on balls getting past the catcher.)

DRA is set to the scale of runs allowed per nine innings (RA9) instead of ERA, which makes DRA's scale slightly higher than ERA's. Because of this, for ease of use, we're supplying DRA-, which is much easier for the reader to parse. As with DRC+, DRA- is an "index" stat, meaning instead of using some arbitrary and shifting number to denote what's "good," average is always 100. The reason that it uses a minus rather than a plus is because like ERA, a lower number is better. Therefore a 75 DRA- describes a performance 25 percent better than average, whereas a 150 DRA- means that either a pitcher is getting extremely lucky with their results, or getting ready to try a new pitch.

Since the last time you picked up an edition of this book, we've also made a few minor changes to DRA to make it better. Recent research into "tunneling"—the act of throwing consecutive pitches that appear similar from a batter's point of view until after the swing decision point–data has given us a new contextual factor to account for in DRA: plate distance. This refers to the distance between successive pitches as they approach the plate, and while it has a smaller effect than factors like velocity or whiff rate, it still can help explain pitcher strikeout rate in our model.

Recently Added Descriptive Statistics

Returning to our 2021 edition of the book are a few figures which recently appeared. These numbers may be a little bit more familiar to those of you who have spent some time investigating baseball statistics.

Fastball Percentage

Our fastball percentage (FA%) statistic measures how frequently a pitcher throws a pitch classified as a "fastball," measured as a percentage of overall pitches thrown. We qualify three types of fastballs:

1. The traditional four-seam fastball;
2. The two-seam fastball or sinker;
3. "Hard cutters," which are pitches that have the movement profile of a cut fastball and are used as the pitcher's primary offering or in place of a more traditional fastball.

For example, a pitcher with a FA% of 67 throws any combination of these three pitches about two-thirds of the time.

Whiff Rate

Everybody loves a swing and a miss, and whiff rate (Whiff%) measures how frequently pitchers induce a swinging strike. To calculate Whiff%, we add up all the pitches thrown that ended with a swinging strike, then divide that number by a pitcher's total pitches thrown. Most often, high whiff rates correlate with high strikeout rates (and overall effective pitcher performance).

Called Strike Probability

Called Strike Probability (CSP) is a number that represents the likelihood that all of a pitcher's pitches will be called a strike while controlling for location, pitcher and batter handedness, umpire and count. Here's how it works: on each pitch, our model determines how many times (out of 100) that a similar pitch was called for a strike given those factors mentioned above, and when normalized for each batter's strike zone. Then we average the CSP for all pitches thrown by a pitcher in a season, and that gives us the yearly CSP percentage you see in the stats boxes.

As you might imagine, pitchers with a higher CSP are more likely to work in the zone, where pitchers with a lower CSP are likely locating their pitches outside the normal strike zone, for better or for worse.

Projections

Many of you aren't turning to this book just for a look at what a player has done, but for a look at what a player is going to do: the PECOTA projections. PECOTA, initially developed by Nate Silver (who has moved on to greater fame as a political analyst), consists of three parts:

1. Major-league equivalencies, which use minor-league statistics to project how a player will perform in the major leagues;
2. Baseline forecasts, which use weighted averages and regression to the mean to estimate a player's current true talent level; and
3. Aging curves, which uses the career paths of comparable players to estimate how a player's statistics are likely to change over time.

With all those important things covered, let's take a look at what's in the book this year.

Team Prospectus

Most of this book is composed of team chapters, with one for each of the 30 major-league franchises. On the first page of each chapter, you'll see a box that contains some of the key statistics for each team as well as a very inviting stadium diagram.

We start with the team name, their unadjusted 2020 win-loss record, and their divisional ranking. Beneath that are a host of other team statistics. **Pythag** presents an adjusted 2020 winning percentage, calculated by taking runs scored per game (**RS/G**) and runs allowed per game (**RA/G**) for the team, and running them through a version of Bill James' Pythagorean formula that was refined and improved by David Smyth and Brandon Heipp. (The formula is called "Pythagenpat," which is equally fun to type and to say.)

Next up is **DRC+**, described earlier, to indicate the overall hitting ability of the team either above or below league-average. Run prevention on the pitching side is covered by **DRA** (also mentioned earlier) and another metric: Fielding Independent Pitching (**FIP**), which calculates another ERA-like statistic based on strikeouts, walks, and home runs recorded. Defensive Efficiency Rating (**DER**) tells us the percentage of balls in play turned into outs for the team, and is a quick fielding shorthand that rounds out run prevention.

After that, we have several measures related to roster composition, as opposed to on-field performance. **B-Age** and **P-Age** tell us the average age of a team's batters and pitchers, respectively. **Payroll** is the combined team payroll for all on-field players, and Doug Pappas' Marginal Dollars per Marginal Win (**M$/MW**) tells us how much money a team spent to earn production above replacement level.

Next to each of these stats, we've listed each team's MLB rank in that category from first to 30th. In this, first always indicates a positive outcome and 30th a negative outcome, except in the case of salary—first is highest.

After the franchise statistics, we share a few items about the team's home ballpark. There's the aforementioned diagram of the park's dimensions (including distances to the outfield wall), a graphic showing the height of the wall from the left-field pole to the right-field pole, and a table showing three-year park factors for the stadium. The park factors are displayed as indexes where 100 is average, 110 means that the park inflates the statistic in question by 10 percent, and 90 means that the park deflates the statistic in question by 10 percent.

On the second page of each team chapter, you'll find three graphs. The first is **Payroll History** and helps you see how the team's payroll has compared to the MLB and divisional average payrolls over time. Payroll figures are current as of January 1, 2021; with so many free agents still unsigned as of this writing, the final 2021 figure will likely be significantly different for many teams. (In the meantime, you can always find the most current data at Baseball Prospectus' Cot's Baseball Contracts page.)

The second graph is **Future Commitments** and helps you see the team's future outlays, if any.

The third graph is **Farm System Ranking** and displays how the Baseball Prospectus prospect team has ranked the organization's farm system since 2007.

After the graphs, we have a **Personnel** section that lists many of the important decision-makers and upper-level field and operations staff members for the franchise, as well as any former Baseball Prospectus staff members who are currently part of the organization. (In very rare circumstances, someone might be on both lists!)

Position Players

After all that information and a thoughtful bylined essay covering each team, we present our player comments. These are also bylined, but due to frequent franchise shifts during the offseason, our bylines are more a rough guide than a perfect accounting of who wrote what.

Each player is listed with the major-league team that employed him as of early January 2021. If a player changed teams after that point via free agency, trade, or any other method, you'll be able to find them in the chapter for their previous squad.

As an example, take a look at the player comment for Padres shortstop Fernando Tatis Jr.: the stat block that accompanies his written comment is at the top of this page. First we cover biographical information (age is as of June 30, 2021) before moving onto the stats themselves. Our statistic columns include standard identifying information like **YEAR**, **TEAM**, **LVL** (level of affiliated play) and **AGE** before getting into the numbers. Next, we provide raw, untranslated

Fernando Tatis Jr. SS

Born: 01/02/99   Age: 22   Bats: R   Throws: R
Height: 6'3"   Weight: 217   Origin: International Free Agent, 2015

YEAR	TEAM	LVL	AGE	PA	R	2B	3B	HR	RBI	BB	K	SB	CS	AVG/OBP/SLG
2018	SA	AA	19	394	77	22	4	16	43	33	109	16	5	.286/.355/.507
2019	SD	MLB	20	372	61	13	6	22	53	30	110	16	6	.317/.379/.590
2020	SD	MLB	21	257	50	11	2	17	45	27	61	11	3	.277/.366/.571
2021 FS	SD	MLB	22	600	95	24	4	31	81	50	165	17	8	.263/.331/.499
2021 DC	SD	MLB	22	628	100	25	4	32	85	53	173	19	8	.263/.331/.499

Comparables: Darryl Strawberry, Bo Bichette, Ronald Acuña Jr.

YEAR	TEAM	LVL	AGE	PA	DRC+	BABIP	BRR	FRAA	WARP
2018	SA	AA	19	394	136	.370	3.0	SS(83): -1.9	2.4
2019	SD	MLB	20	372	118	.410	7.1	SS(83): 0.9	3.4
2020	SD	MLB	21	257	126	.306	0.7	SS(57): -5.5	0.9
2021 FS	SD	MLB	22	600	126	.318	1.7	SS -1	3.9
2021 DC	SD	MLB	22	628	126	.318	1.8	SS -1	4.0

numbers like you might find on the back of your dad's baseball cards: **PA** (plate appearances), **R** (runs), **2B** (doubles), **3B** (triples), **HR** (home runs), **RBI** (runs batted in), **BB** (walks), **K** (strikeouts), **SB** (stolen bases) and **CS** (caught stealing).

Following the basic stats is **Whiff%** (whiff rate), which denotes how often, when a batter swings, he fails to make contact with the ball. Another way to think of this number is an inverse of a hitter's contact rate.

Next, we have unadjusted "slash" statistics: **AVG** (batting average), **OBP** (on-base percentage) and **SLG** (slugging percentage). Following the slash line is **DRC+** (Deserved Runs Created Plus), which we described earlier as total offensive expected contribution compared to the league average.

BABIP (batting average on balls in play) tells us how often a ball in play fell for a hit, and can help us identify whether a batter may have been lucky or not ... but note that high BABIPs also tend to follow the great hitters of our time, as well as speedy singles hitters who put the ball on the ground.

The next item is **BRR** (Baserunning Runs), which covers all of a player's baserunning accomplishments including (but not limited to) swiped bags and failed attempts. Next is **FRAA** (Fielding Runs Above Average), which also includes the number of games previously played at each position noted in parentheses. Multi-position players have only their two most frequent positions listed here, but their total FRAA number reflects all positions played.

Our last column here is **WARP** (Wins Above Replacement Player). WARP estimates the total value of a player, which means for hitters it takes into account hitting runs above average (calculated using the DRC+ model), BRR and FRAA. Then, it makes an adjustment for positions played and gives the player a credit

Milwaukee Brewers 2021

for plate appearances based upon the difference between "replacement level"—which is derived from the quality of players added to a team's roster after the start of the season–and the league average.

The final line just below the stats box is **PECOTA** data, which is discussed further in a following section.

Catchers

Catchers are a special breed, and thus they have earned their own separate box which displays some of the defensive metrics that we've built just for them. As an example, let's check out Yasmani Grandal.

YEAR	TEAM	P. COUNT	FRM RUNS	BLK RUNS	THRW RUNS	TOT RUNS
2018	LAD	16816	15.7	0.8	0.1	16.5
2019	MIL	18740	19.4	1.8	-0.1	21.1
2020	CHW	4830	3.7	0.3	-0.2	3.8
2021	CHW	14430	16.7	-0.6	1.0	17.1
2021	CHW	14430	16.7	0.4	1.0	18.0

The **YEAR** and **TEAM** columns match what you'd find in the other stat box. **P. COUNT** indicates the number of pitches thrown while the catcher was behind the plate, including swinging strikes, fouls and balls in play. **FRM RUNS** is the total run value the catcher provided (or cost) his team by influencing the umpire to call strikes where other catchers did not. **BLK RUNS** expresses the total run value above or below average for the catcher's ability to prevent wild pitches and passed balls. **THRW RUNS** is calculated using a similar model as the previous two statistics, and it measures a catcher's ability to throw out basestealers but also to dissuade them from testing his arm in the first place. It takes into account factors like the pitcher (including his delivery and pickoff move) and baserunner (who could be as fast as Billy Hamilton or as slow as Yonder Alonso). **TOT RUNS** is the sum of all of the previous three statistics.

Pitchers

Let's give our pitchers a turn, using 2020 AL Cy Young winner Shane Bieber as our example. Take a look at his stat block: the first line and the **YEAR**, **TEAM**, **LVL** and **AGE** columns are the same as in the position player example earlier.

Here too, we have a series of columns that display raw, unadjusted statistics compiled by the pitcher over the course of a season: **W** (wins), **L** (losses), **SV** (saves), **G** (games pitched), **GS** (games started), **IP** (innings pitched), **H** (hits allowed) and **HR** (home runs allowed). Next we have two statistics that are rates: **BB/9** (walks per nine innings) and **K/9** (strikeouts per nine innings), before returning to the unadjusted K (strikeouts).

Next up is **GB%** (ground ball percentage), which is the percentage of all batted balls that were hit on the ground, including both outs and hits. Remember, this is based on observational data and subject to human error, so please approach this with a healthy dose of skepticism.

BABIP (batting average on balls in play) is calculated using the same methodology as it is for position players, but it often tells us more about a pitcher than it does a hitter. With pitchers, a high BABIP is often due to poor defense or bad luck, and can often be an indicator of potential rebound, and a low BABIP may be cause to expect performance regression. (A typical league-average BABIP is close to .290-.300.)

The metrics **WHIP** (walks plus hits per inning pitched) and **ERA** (earned run average) are old standbys: WHIP measures walks and hits allowed on a per-inning basis, while ERA measures earned runs on a nine-inning basis. Neither of these stats are translated or adjusted.

DRA- (Deserved Run Average) was described at length earlier, and measures how the pitcher "deserved" to perform compared to other pitchers. Please note that since we lack all the data points that would make for a "real" DRA for minor-league events, the DRA- displayed for minor league partial-seasons is based off of different data. (That data is a modified version of our cFIP metric, which you can find more information about on our website.)

Shane Bieber RHP

Born: 05/31/95 Age: 26 Bats: R Throws: R
Height: 6'3" Weight: 200 Origin: Round 4, 2016 Draft (#122 overall)

YEAR	TEAM	LVL	AGE	W	L	SV	G	GS	IP	H	HR	BB/9	K/9	K	GB%	BABIP
2018	AKR	AA	23	3	0	0	5	5	31	26	1	0.3	8.7	30	47.3%	.278
2018	COL	AAA	23	3	1	0	8	8	48[2]	30	3	1.1	8.7	47	52.0%	.227
2018	CLE	MLB	23	11	5	0	20	19	114[2]	130	13	1.8	9.3	118	46.2%	.356
2019	CLE	MLB	24	15	8	0	34	33	214[1]	186	31	1.7	10.9	259	44.4%	.298
2020	CLE	MLB	25	8	1	0	12	12	77[1]	46	7	2.4	14.2	122	48.4%	.267
2021 FS	CLE	MLB	26	10	6	0	26	26	150	121	18	2.1	11.7	195	45.5%	.297
2021 DC	CLE	MLB	26	14	7	0	30	30	196.7	159	24	2.1	11.7	257	45.5%	.297

Comparables: Luis Severino, Danny Salazar, Joe Musgrove

YEAR	TEAM	LVL	AGE	WHIP	ERA	DRA-	WARP	MPH	FB%	WHF	CSP
2018	AKR	AA	23	0.87	1.16	61	0.9				
2018	COL	AAA	23	0.74	1.66	69	1.2				
2018	CLE	MLB	23	1.33	4.55	74	2.6	94.7	57.4%	26.2%	
2019	CLE	MLB	24	1.05	3.28	75	4.9	94.4	45.8%	30.8%	
2020	CLE	MLB	25	0.87	1.63	53	2.6	95.3	53.6%	40.7%	
2021 FS	CLE	MLB	26	1.04	2.44	64	4.4	94.7	50.0%	33.2%	44.2%
2021 DC	CLE	MLB	26	1.04	2.44	64	5.8	94.7	50.0%	33.2%	44.2%

Just like with hitters, **WARP** (Wins Above Replacement Player) is a total value metric that puts pitchers of all stripes on the same scale as position players. We use DRA as the primary input for our calculation of WARP. You might notice that relief pitchers (due to their limited innings) may have a lower WARP than you were expecting or than you might see in other WARP-like metrics. WARP does not take leverage into account, just the actions a pitcher performs and the expected value of those actions ... which ends up judging high-leverage relief pitchers differently than you might imagine given their prestige and market value.

MPH gives you the pitcher's 95th percentile velocity for the noted season, in order to give you an idea of what the *peak* fastball velocity a pitcher possesses. Since this comes from our pitch-tracking data, it is not publicly available for minor-league pitchers.

Finally, we display the three new pitching metrics we described earlier. **FB%** (fastball percentage) gives you the percentage of fastballs thrown out of all pitches. **WHF** (whiff rate) tells you the percentage of swinging strikes induced out of all pitches. **CSP** (called strike probability) expresses the likelihood of all pitches thrown to result in a called strike, after controlling for factors like handedness, umpire, pitch type, count and location.

PECOTA

All players have PECOTA projections for 2021, as well as a set of other numbers that describe the performance of comparable players according to PECOTA. All projections for 2021 are for the player at the date we went to press in early January and are projected into the league and park context as indicated by the team abbreviation. (Note that players at very low levels of the minors are too unpredictable to assess using these numbers.) All PECOTA projected statistics represent a player's projected major-league performance.

How we're doing that is a little different this season. There are really two different values that go into the final stat line that you see for PECOTA: How a player performs, and how much playing time he'll be given to perform it. In the past we've estimated playing time based on each team's roster and depth charts, and we'll continue to do that. These projections are denoted as **2021 DC**.

But in many cases, a player won't be projected for major-league playing time; most of the time this is because they aren't projected to be major-league players at all, but still developing as prospects. Or perhaps a player will provide Triple-A depth, only to have an opportunity open up because of injury. For these purposes, we're also supplying a second projection, labeled **2021 FS**, or full season. This is what we would project the player to provide in 600 plate appearances or 150 innings pitched.

Below the projections are the player's three highest-scoring comparable players as determined by PECOTA. All comparables represent a snapshot of how the listed player was performing at the same age as the current player, so if a

23-year-old pitcher is compared to Bartolo Colón, he's actually being compared to a 23-year-old Colón, not the version that pitched for the Rangers in 2018, nor to Colón's career as a whole.

A few points about pitcher projections. First, we aren't yet projecting peak velocity, so that column will be blank in the PECOTA lines. Second, projecting DRA is trickier than evaluating past performance, because it is unclear how deserving each pitcher will be of his anticipated outcomes. However, we know that another DRA-related statistic–contextual FIP or cFIP-estimates future run scoring very well. So for PECOTA, the projected DRA- figures you see are based on the past cFIPs generated by the pitcher and comparable players over time, along with the other factors described above.

If you're familiar with PECOTA, then you'll have noticed that the projection system often appears bullish on players coming off a bad year and bearish on players coming off a good year. (This is because the system weights several previous seasons, not just the most recent one.) In addition, we publish the 50th percentile projections for each player–which is smack in the middle of the range of projected production—which tends to mean PECOTA stat lines don't often have extreme results like 40 home runs or 250 strikeouts in a given season. In essence, PECOTA doesn't project very many extreme seasons.

Managers

After all those wonderful team chapters, we've got statistics for each big-league manager, all of whom are organized by alphabetical order. Here you'll find a block including an extraordinary amount of information collected from each manager's entire career. For more information on the acronyms and what they mean, please visit the Glossary at www.baseballprospectus.com.

There is one important metric that we'd like to call attention to, and you'll find it next to each manager's name: **wRM+** (weighted reliever management plus). Developed by Rob Arthur and Rian Watt, wRM+ investigates how good a manager is at using their best relievers during the moments of highest leverage, using both our proprietary DRA metric as well as Leverage Index. wRM+ is scaled to a league average of 100, and a wRM+ of 105 indicates that relievers were used approximately five percent "better" than average. On the other hand, a wRM+ of 95 would tell us the team used its relievers five percent "worse" than the average team.

While wRM+ does not have an extremely strong correlation with a manager, it is statistically significant; this means that a manager is not *entirely* responsible for a team's wRM+, but does have some effect on that number.

Part 1: Team Analysis

Performance Graphs

Payroll History (in millions)

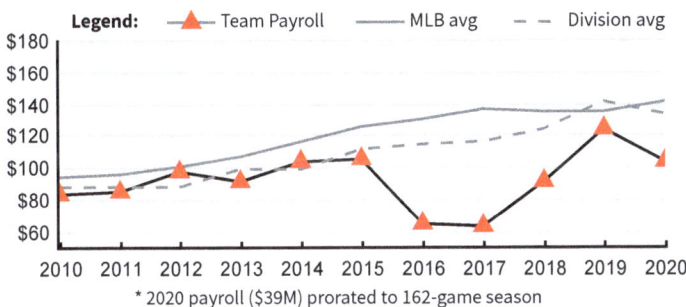

* 2020 payroll ($39M) prorated to 162-game season

Future Commitments (in millions)

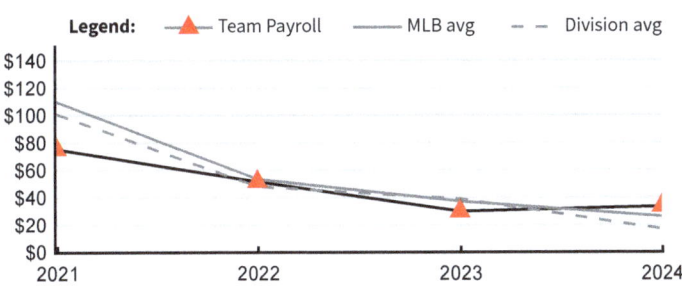

Farm System Ranking

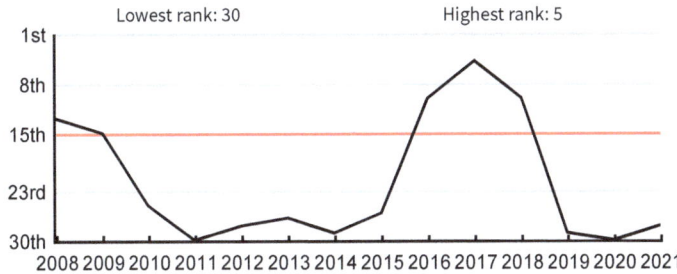

2020 Team Performance

ACTUAL STANDINGS

Team	W	L	Pct
CHC	34	26	0.567
CIN	31	29	0.517
STL	30	28	0.517
MIL	**29**	**31**	**0.483**
PIT	19	41	0.317

dWIN% STANDINGS

Team	W	L	Pct
CIN	32	28	0.537
MIL	**29**	**31**	**0.496**
CHC	27	33	0.465
STL	26	34	0.436
PIT	20	40	0.344

TOP HITTERS

Player	WARP
Orlando Arcia	0.7
Eric Sogard	0.6
Jedd Gyorko	0.4

TOP PITCHERS

Player	WARP
Brandon Woodruff	1.9
Corbin Burnes	1.8
Devin Williams	1.1

VITAL STATISTICS

Statistic Name	Value	Rank
Pythagenpat	.469	18th
dWin%	.496	12th
Runs Scored per Game	4.12	27th
Runs Allowed per Game	4.40	11th
Deserved Runs Created Plus	93	25th
Deserved Run Average Minus	87	4th
Fielding Independent Pitching	3.86	4th
Defensive Efficiency Rating	.690	23rd
Batter Age	28.9	9th
Pitcher Age	28.2	10th
Payroll	$39.0M	24th
Marginal $ per Marginal Win	$1.9M	8th

2021 Team Projections

PROJECTED STANDINGS

Team	W	L	Pct	+/-
MIL	89.1	72.9	0.550	10
Adding Kolten Wong doesn't quite make this an above-average lineup, but it improves their run prevention. Playoff hopes hinge on Christian Yelich being himself again.				
CHC	84.9	77.1	0.524	-6
Change, though painful, will give them an overdue chance to evaluate new options.				
STL	80.4	81.6	0.496	0
Nolan Arenado makes them favorites in the NL Central, but real parity with the goliaths on the coasts is still a ways off.				
CIN	79.3	82.7	0.490	-4
Traded or non-tendered several key role players to save money, and their Cy Young winner left as a free agent.				
PIT	59.5	102.5	0.367	8
This year will be about sorting out shortstop, hoping for progress from Mitch Keller, and enjoying Ke'Bryan Hayes--but not much more.				

TOP PROJECTED HITTERS

Player	WARP
Christian Yelich	3.9
Kolten Wong	3.0
Lorenzo Cain	2.2

TOP PROJECTED PITCHERS

Player	WARP
Brandon Woodruff	3.9
Corbin Burnes	2.3
Brent Suter	2.2

FARM SYSTEM REPORT

Top Prospect	Number of Top 101 Prospects
Brice Turang	0

KEY DEDUCTIONS

Player	WARP
Corey Knebel	0.6
Alex Claudio	0.4

KEY ADDITIONS

Player	WARP
Kolten Wong	3.0
Lorenzo Cain	2.2
Daniel Robertson	0.5

Team Personnel

President - Baseball Operations
David Stearns

Senior Vice President and General Manager
Matt Arnold

Senior Vice President - Player Personnel
Karl Mueller

Manager
Craig Counsell

BP Alumni
James Fisher
Adam Hayes
Mike Groopman
Shawn Hoffman
Matt Kleine
Dan Turkenkopf
Andrew Koo

Miller Park Stats

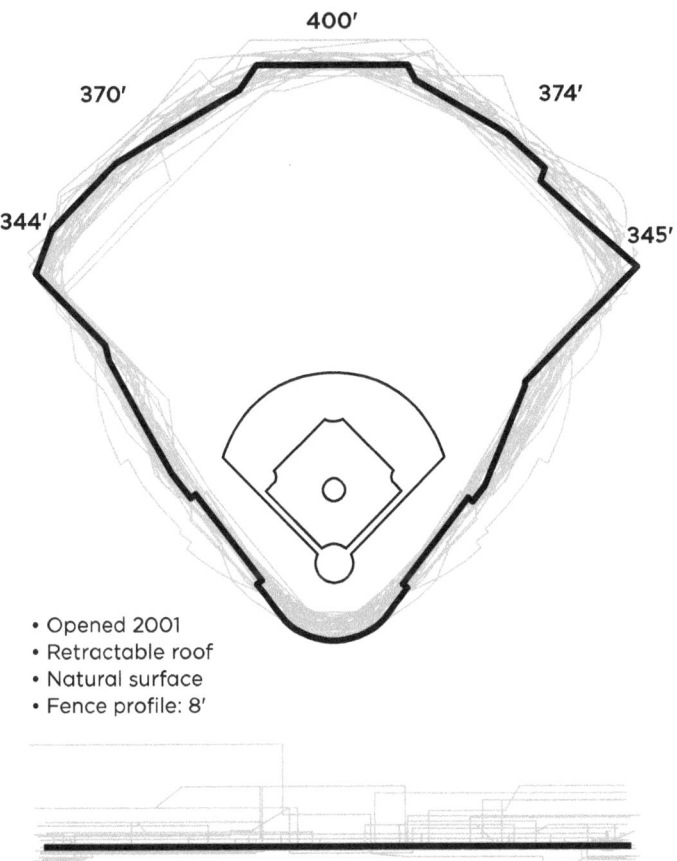

- Opened 2001
- Retractable roof
- Natural surface
- Fence profile: 8'

Three-Year Park Factors

Runs	Runs/RH	Runs/LH	HR/RH	HR/LH
102	103	101	104	105

Brewers Team Analysis

Officially, the Milwaukee Brewers did not cease play on September 14; they continued on into the playoffs, until they were sent home by the eventual champion Los Angeles Dodgers in quick order. You can still forgive any Brewers fan who watched that day's action—a doubleheader against the St. Louis Cardinals—and walked away without optimism for the weeks ahead. That void of hope wasn't the team's results (they split the pair), but the play of Christian Yelich, Milwaukee's bellwether. Yelich went 1 for 8 with six strikeouts on the day. Both games ranked among his four worst of the season, as judged by Baseball Reference's Win Probability Added.

Seeing Yelich swing through Daniel Ponce de Leon fastballs was disheartening, but the day's enduring image was when he swung over a Genesis Cabrera breaking ball, his eyes drawn back to the catcher's mitt with his bat still pointed skyward. Yelich, as he started toward the dugout, signaled his own disappointment with a universal sign of frustration: he rotated his shoulders quickly—the way one might if they missed out on the lottery by a single digit, or if they forgot to tape their favorite show. He held the pose for several strides, until he was nearly out of view (and, in 2020 terms, off the stage).

It was that kind of year for both Yelich and the Brewers. Milwaukee reached the playoffs for a third year in a row but they did so on a technicality; through the generosity of the expanded postseason bracket, and a losing record. What's worse is they did it with the realization that baseball—and, indeed, life—can change quickly, and not always for the better. There are few better examples of that reality than Milwaukee's relationship with Yelich.

⚾   ⚾   ⚾

Too often these days, it feels as though big-league teams are forcing themselves to choose between being in the money-making business or being in the winning business. No one but billionaires thinks those two things are actually in conflict, but the distinction has defined seasons for a number of teams recently, and at times it can seem to define the league as a whole. The Brewers, as the smallest-market team (depending on how you count these things), ostensibly face as much pressure as anyone to choose one of those paradigms. Instead, since last March, they've staked out their own path by going all-in on the Christian Yelich business.

When president of baseball operations David Stearns acquired Yelich in January 2018, he and his front office paid a handsome price. Even at the time, it was clear that Yelich had untapped potential, but that wasn't the primary reason his price tag was so high. More than his relative youth or his athleticism or his impressive hard-hit rate, Yelich's contract made him the Marlins outfielder in the greatest demand. When the Brewers obtained the rights to his services, they did so for up to five seasons, at a total cost of no more than $58.25 million. Yelich's then-teammates, Giancarlo Stanton and Marcell Ozuna, were coming off MVP and career seasons—the kind of years teams could only hope for from Yelich. Yet Yelich had the highest trade value of the three, and brought the most back, because of finances.

One year later, Yelich had more than made good on his upside, with a historic second half that vaulted him to a well-deserved MVP award of his own. Another year on, he'd come within a fluke September injury of repeating, and yet the Brewers still had him under their control for three seasons at less than $42 million. This is why teams adore early-career extensions like the one to which the Marlins inked Yelich in March 2015: they create massive upside for the team, lend them cost certainty, and hardly ever lose value, except in the final year or two before an especially disappointing player hits free agency.

As great as Yelich had proved himself to be, he turned 28 prior to the 2020 season, meaning that he'd be 30 in 2022 and would effectively hit free agency at 31, after making $15 million that year. Even superstars are often in noticeable decline by the time they reach 31, and Yelich is a corner outfielder who (for all the other dazzling things about his prior two seasons) has already lost a step or two defensively. For a team operating on a purely cost- and flexibility-conscious model, letting Yelich play out the string on that deal would have been the obvious move.

Instead, the Brewers behaved in a proactive manner with Yelich, signing him to a new long-term contract roughly a week before the coronavirus pandemic shut the sport down. The new deal extended the Brewers' control of Yelich through 2029. It preserved his salaries for 2020 and 2021, but beginning in 2022 (when the Brewers had that $15-million option on him), it gave him a raise to $26 million per year. Yelich will make that much all the way through 2028, with a mutual option at the end of the deal worth another $20 million.

The contract hasn't kicked in yet, but the Brewers might already have some concerns.

Yelich's 2020 was its own kind of pain for a team so invested in a particular player. There's little reason to be overly concerned, but he struggled in a real way amid the bizarre circumstances of the season, and in his first action since suffering a fractured kneecap. He fanned nearly 31 percent of the time, so while he did hit into bad luck (his .259 batting average on balls in play was the lowest of his career by nearly 70 points despite a career-high exit velocity), one can't chalk his struggles up to that alone. The graceful, lethal swing he'd honed so perfectly over the previous two years, with its exquisitely-controlled violence, only showed up in flashes and he wasn't confident enough in it to trigger it with the necessary frequency. Too many deep counts inevitably led to strikeouts, and even though he hit the ball as hard as ever, there were too many counts in which that hard contact was impossible or easily defended.

Last season showed that, like other teams who have double-downed with a player whose first team-friendly contract turned out especially well (the Rays, with Evan Longoria; the Brewers themselves, with Ryan Braun; the Tigers, with Miguel Cabrera; the Nationals with Ryan Zimmerman; and others), the Brewers are especially exposed if Yelich turns downhill more quickly than expected. With the deferrals to which Yelich agreed, the Brewers will be making seven-figure payments to him at least into the early 2040s.

Last season also highlighted the conflict that will define the Brewers' next decade: Can they build a winner around Yelich, and, if so, how can they pull that off when neither their budget nor their farm system figures to offer relief?

⚾ ⚾ ⚾

The Brewers have made a habit out of flouting their abnormal tolerance for risk to maximize their chances: they've traded their last two competitive-balance draft picks for affordable big-league role players; they've dealt role players for unusually far-off players, clearing the low-dollar contracts attached to vets like Adam Lind and David Phelps, plus adding entry-level minor-leaguers (again) without paying their signing bonuses. Milwaukee will save a buck wherever they can, especially if it doesn't wholly short-circuit their competitive aspirations.

The trades they use to thread the needle of acquiring young players might be a bit offensive to our sensibilities, but the opportunity costs involved are minimal, and they've proved to be able to get real value out of those moves. They have operated, especially over the last two years, like a team deeply concerned with having good, young talent at hand, but far less so with boasting a top-ranked farm system. Their pipeline has some players, even now, who will sneak up on teams. They just don't have the prospect capital to pull off another Yelich-type deal. For most franchises, and certainly for this one, that's a once-in-a-generation trade. (Keeping that in mind helps one understand the team's decision to double down on their MVP in the first place.)

The Brewers, as a result, have to suffer risk in ways that other teams might take for granted. Keeping both Brandon Woodruff and Corbin Burnes in the starting rotation, given their profiles and the adversity each had encountered, looked like a bit of a stretch. The Brewers did it anyway and now they have two front-end starters with exceptional stuff. In the bullpen, where they continue to tolerate and even foster certain things other teams would never permit, the team keeps finding gems. In 2020, that was Rookie of the Year winner Devin Williams, a frustrating, injury-hampered first-round pick who more than made good after learning a screwball. (He calls it a changeup.) Josh Hader continues apace at the back end, not quite at the levels of durability or brilliance he achieved when he first entered the majors, but still very much a dominating closer. The team still asks relievers to get more than three outs at an unusual rate (they ranked 11th in the majors in that regard); still embraces strange arm angles and deliveries and still seems to get more out of their pen than most of their rivals do, either in spite of or because of their risk tolerance.

One problem with Milwaukee's approach is that risks are deemed risks for a reason. We know from research (and from experience) that even the savviest risk taker fails—a lot. The Brewers sure did, so far as it pertained to their 2020 lineup. Hence Justin Smoak and Brock Holt being handed their walking papers before the season ended; hence Omar Narváez and Eric Sogard falling flat; hence waiver-claim Daniel Vogelbach being given a late-season opportunity. (The Brewers *did* hit on Jedd Gyorko, but they surprisingly declined his option to begin the winter.)

Another problem is that the Brewers' risks were almost certain to be low-yield. The exception was handing Avisaíl García a two-year pact worth $20 million (plus a club option) in exchange for the opportunity to see if Milwaukee could unlock his long-rumored upside. García's first season in town went poorly—he had his worst offensive showing in years—but at least there was a ceiling on the transaction. Too many of the Brewers' other gambles lacked one.

Moving forward, the need is obvious. The mandate is even more so. The question is: With few prospects to trade, will the Brewers have the guts to wade into free agency and make some expensive additions to their core? From a divisional perspective, this might be the ideal time for Milwaukee to push its chips to the middle: the Cardinals are aging; the Cubs and the Reds are bailing on competing; the Pirates are the Pirates. The Brewers are, not to be literal, the wild card.

Being in the Yelich business means making the most of his prime, which is happening right now. This team was aggressive in consecutive winters not so long ago, signing Cain to that five-year, $85-million deal the same year they traded for Yelich, then inking Yasmani Grandal and Mike Moustakas to bargain deals after 2018. That was during two historically frigid offseasons. The next few winters figure to be chilly as well, as the league adjusts to the impact the COVID-19 pandemic has had (and will have) on revenues while keeping a little in the coffers in case of a work stoppage in 2022.

Undeniably, the pandemic hurt every big-league team, and it hurt the Brewers even more than most. The team's local TV rights are not the bonanza others' are, making the team highly reliant on game-day revenues. The culture the club has created within its community has generally made that perfectly viable, but in a season without fans, they felt an especially acute pain.

Still, the uncertainty that waits around the bend presents the Brewers with an opportunity—the team that loves to take chances should embrace what other teams might consider to be the loftiest risk: spending money. Milwaukee has seemed to satisfy itself with taking a large number of small gambles, instead of being opportunistic and aiming high. That strategy is incompatible with the broader, Yelich-focused business model. The Brewers, then, would be wise to go back to the playbook that netted them Cain, Grandal, Moustakas and even Yelich himself.

The extraordinarily high floor for revenue set by national TV-rights deals; the promise of multiple effective, safe COVID-19 vaccines; and Yelich's new deal make the team's best way forward clear: spend some money, build a thunderous lineup around a player who might wear the ball-and-glove logo on a plaque in Cooperstown someday and take advantage of a soft NL Central over the next half-decade. Milwaukee shouldn't be in the business of doing anything less.

—*Matthew Trueblood is an author of Baseball Prospectus.*

Part 2: Player Analysis

PLAYER COMMENTS WITH GRAPHS

Orlando Arcia SS
Born: 08/04/94   Age: 26   Bats: R   Throws: R
Height: 6'0"   Weight: 187   Origin: International Free Agent, 2010

YEAR	TEAM	LVL	AGE	PA	R	2B	3B	HR	RBI	BB	K	SB	CS	AVG/OBP/SLG
2018	RMV	AAA	23	96	16	5	1	2	8	10	15	2	1	.341/.417/.494
2018	MIL	MLB	23	366	32	16	0	3	30	15	87	7	4	.236/.268/.307
2019	MIL	MLB	24	546	51	16	1	15	59	43	109	8	5	.223/.283/.350
2020	MIL	MLB	25	189	22	10	1	5	20	14	32	2	0	.260/.317/.416
2021 FS	MIL	MLB	26	600	69	24	2	16	74	42	122	11	5	.250/.305/.395
2021 DC	MIL	MLB	26	539	62	22	2	15	66	37	109	9	5	.250/.305/.395

Comparables: Jason Donald, JT Riddle, Leo Cardenas

"Insofar as the clutch hitter is not a sportswriter's myth, he is a vulgarity, like a writer who writes only for money," John Updike wrote in his only published work about baseball. What Arcia's career supposes is, maybe it isn't. Updike, after all, was writing about Ted Williams; the only way for Williams to elevate his game in clutch moments would have been to focus less than he might have in other, lesser moments since pitchers always gave Williams their best when the game was on the line. For Arcia, it's different. If he's giving his usual focus to a big moment, he might gain an edge over pitchers, because their minds are often on the better hitters on the other side of the lineup card. That, perhaps, is how Arcia so often seems to ambush hurlers in high-leverage situations, and how he has (for instance) slugged .568 for his postseason career. (Or, maybe it's blind luck. Either way, he made huge strides at bat in 2020, counterbalancing his defensive decline.)

YEAR	TEAM	LVL	AGE	PA	DRC+	BABIP	BRR	FRAA	WARP
2018	RMV	AAA	23	96	130	.397	2.3	SS(22): 3.9	1.3
2018	MIL	MLB	23	366	58	.305	2.0	SS(116): 3.8	0.4
2019	MIL	MLB	24	546	74	.253	-0.7	SS(150): -2.3	0.5
2020	MIL	MLB	25	189	96	.292	-0.4	SS(57): 3.2, P(2): -0.0, CF(1): -0.1	0.7
2021 FS	MIL	MLB	26	600	91	.292	0.5	SS 2, 1B 0	1.4
2021 DC	MIL	MLB	26	539	91	.292	0.4	SS 2	1.2

Orlando Arcia, continued

Batted Ball Distribution

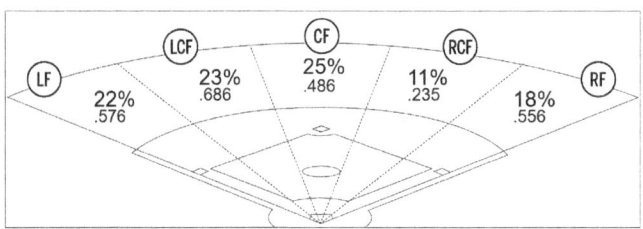

Strike Zone vs LHP

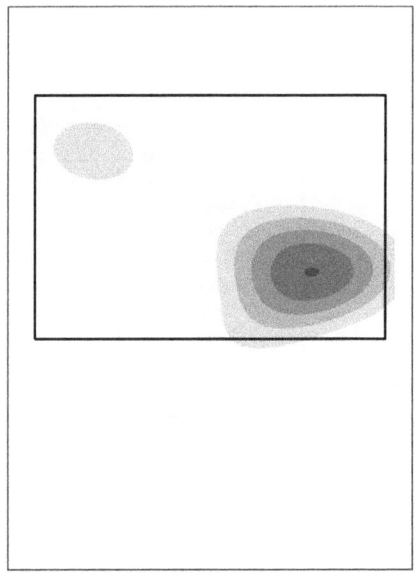

Strike Zone vs RHP

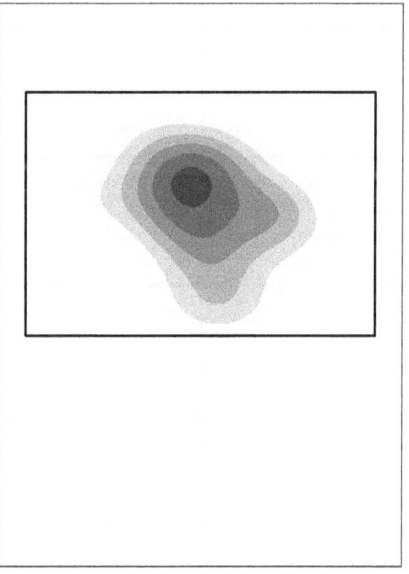

Type	Frequency	Velocity	H Movement	V Movement
● Fastball	26.7%	73.5 [39]	-8.2 [93]	-31.9 [53]
▲ Changeup	66.7%	52.2 [-29]	1.3 [169]	-79.8 [-44]

Brewers Player Analysis - 17

Milwaukee Brewers 2021

Ryan Braun LF

Born: 11/17/83 Age: 37 Bats: R Throws: R
Height: 6'2" Weight: 205 Origin: Round 1, 2005 Draft (#5 overall)

YEAR	TEAM	LVL	AGE	PA	R	2B	3B	HR	RBI	BB	K	SB	CS	AVG/OBP/SLG
2018	MIL	MLB	34	447	59	25	1	20	64	34	85	11	5	.254/.313/.469
2019	MIL	MLB	35	508	70	31	2	22	75	34	105	11	1	.285/.343/.505
2020	MIL	MLB	36	141	14	7	1	8	26	7	27	1	0	.233/.281/.488
2021 FS	MIL	MLB	37	600	69	26	1	25	79	46	136	15	5	.241/.307/.437
2021 DC	MIL	MLB	37	350	40	15	0	14	46	27	79	8	3	.241/.307/.437

Comparables: George Foster, Matt Holliday, Ryan Klesko

This is, in all likelihood, the valedictory comment for Ryan Braun. He'll remain a controversial figure, but he could absolutely rake, and he is the enduring symbol of an era in which the Brewers returned to regular contender status.

YEAR	TEAM	LVL	AGE	PA	DRC+	BABIP	BRR	FRAA	WARP
2018	MIL	MLB	34	447	107	.274	-0.8	LF(93): -4.9, 1B(18): -0.4, RF(1): -0.2	0.8
2019	MIL	MLB	35	508	110	.325	0.7	LF(110): -7.1, RF(2): -0.2	1.4
2020	MIL	MLB	36	141	106	.232	-1.2	RF(20): 0.6, 1B(1): -0.0	0.3
2021 FS	MIL	MLB	37	600	100	.275	0.8	LF -4, RF 0	1.2
2021 DC	MIL	MLB	37	350	100	.275	0.5	LF -3, RF 0	0.7

Ryan Braun, continued

Batted Ball Distribution

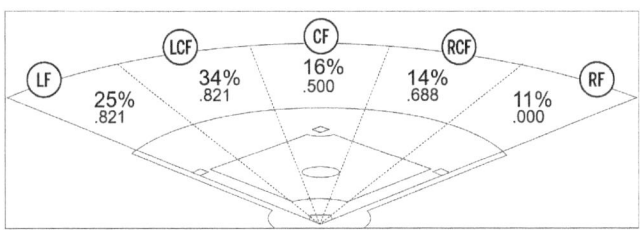

Strike Zone vs LHP Strike Zone vs RHP

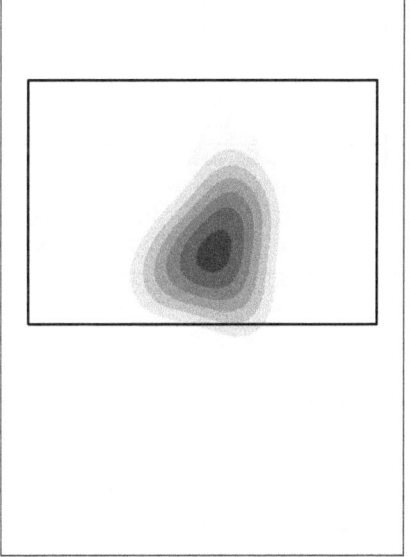

Brewers Player Analysis - 19

Avisaíl García RF

Born: 06/12/91 Age: 30 Bats: R Throws: R
Height: 6'4" Weight: 250 Origin: International Free Agent, 2007

YEAR	TEAM	LVL	AGE	PA	R	2B	3B	HR	RBI	BB	K	SB	CS	AVG/OBP/SLG
2018	CHA	AAA	27	28	5	3	0	3	9	3	9	0	0	.360/.429/.840
2018	CHW	MLB	27	385	47	11	2	19	49	20	102	3	1	.236/.281/.438
2019	TB	MLB	28	530	61	25	2	20	72	31	125	10	4	.282/.332/.464
2020	MIL	MLB	29	207	20	10	0	2	15	20	49	1	3	.238/.333/.326
2021 FS	MIL	MLB	30	600	77	26	1	20	79	44	153	7	3	.253/.320/.420
2021 DC	MIL	MLB	30	565	72	24	1	18	74	41	144	6	3	.253/.320/.420

Comparables: Glenallen Hill, Sammy Sosa, Brennan Boesch

Baseball is most fun to watch when it froths with hustle. García keeps every game in which he plays agitated in just that way. His best physical comp might be mid-career Dave Winfield; it's hard to think of many others who were athletic enough to play the outfield well despite being built like a tight end. He accepted the job of replacing Cain after the veteran center fielder opted out of the season, and he was stretched as an everyday guy in center. Nevertheless, García absolutely barrels after balls, throws well and busts his ass out of the batter's box any time he smells an infield hit. He had a major power outage in 2020, and without the pop he'd finally found over the preceding seasons, he's back to being a second-division starter.

YEAR	TEAM	LVL	AGE	PA	DRC+	BABIP	BRR	FRAA	WARP
2018	CHA	AAA	27	28	130	.462	-0.3	RF(5): -0.2	0.0
2018	CHW	MLB	27	385	98	.271	-1.4	RF(87): 6.3	1.2
2019	TB	MLB	28	530	103	.340	-3.5	RF(92): -3.7, CF(12): 2.1	0.9
2020	MIL	MLB	29	207	93	.315	-0.7	CF(44): -8.9, RF(5): -0.2	-0.5
2021 FS	MIL	MLB	30	600	102	.316	-0.1	RF 1, CF -2	1.4
2021 DC	MIL	MLB	30	565	102	.316	-0.1	RF 1, CF -2	1.3

Avisaíl García, continued

Batted Ball Distribution

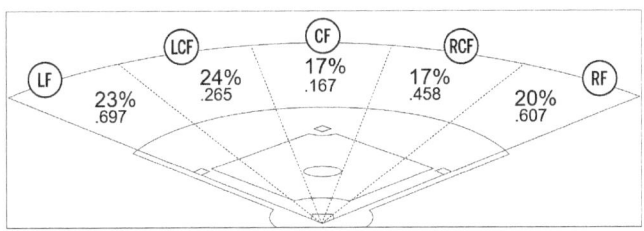

Strike Zone vs LHP   Strike Zone vs RHP

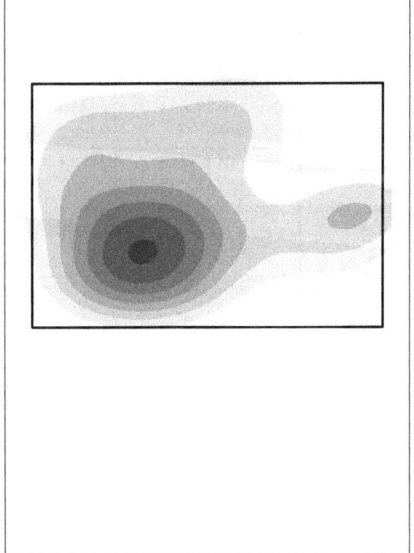

Jedd Gyorko 3B

Born: 09/23/88   Age: 32   Bats: R   Throws: R
Height: 5'10"   Weight: 205   Origin: Round 2, 2010 Draft (#59 overall)

YEAR	TEAM	LVL	AGE	PA	R	2B	3B	HR	RBI	BB	K	SB	CS	AVG/OBP/SLG
2018	STL	MLB	29	402	49	19	1	11	47	44	77	2	0	.262/.346/.416
2019	OKC	AAA	30	26	5	1	0	1	5	3	5	0	0	.273/.385/.455
2019	STL	MLB	30	62	5	0	0	2	7	6	14	2	0	.196/.274/.304
2019	LAD	MLB	30	39	1	1	0	0	2	3	10	0	0	.139/.205/.167
2020	MIL	MLB	31	135	19	3	0	9	17	15	38	0	0	.248/.333/.504
2021 FS	MIL	MLB	32	600	72	19	1	27	81	57	160	3	2	.232/.311/.429

Comparables: Jeff Kent, Neil Walker, Brian Dozier

In the majors, the margins in which a player's season is defined are so thin they can sometimes seem vanishing. That goes almost triple in a 60-game season. Gyorko hit batted balls at 100 or more miles per hour, with a launch angle between 0 and 35 degrees, in about 12 percent of his plate appearances in 2020. For the half-decade prior thereto, he fluctuated between 8 and 11 percent. The difference seems impossibly small because it is, but it led to the best OPS of Gyorko's career thanks in no small part to the small sample in question. (It doesn't hurt, though, that he also showed a bit better plate discipline and continued a recent streak of being well-liked in the clubhouse.) So much of Milwaukee's last offseason went wrong; inking Gyorko to a one-year deal with an option, however, qualified as a win, which is why their decision to decline said option was all the more puzzling.

YEAR	TEAM	LVL	AGE	PA	DRC+	BABIP	BRR	FRAA	WARP
2018	STL	MLB	29	402	109	.303	-1.2	3B(96): -4.8, 2B(17): 0.1, 1B(5): 0.1	1.3
2019	OKC	AAA	30	26	89	.312	-0.8	1B(4): -0.2, 3B(2): -0.1	-0.1
2019	STL	MLB	30	62	78	.225	-0.1	3B(12): 0.5, 2B(2): 0.1, 1B(1): -0.0	0.1
2019	LAD	MLB	30	39	53	.192	-0.3	3B(9): 0.3, 1B(7): -0.8, 2B(1): 0.6	-0.1
2020	MIL	MLB	31	135	108	.278	0.2	1B(30): -1.7, 3B(11): 0.4, P(1): -0.0	0.4
2021 FS	MIL	MLB	32	600	100	.277	-0.5	3B -1, 1B -1	1.0

Jedd Gyorko, continued

Batted Ball Distribution

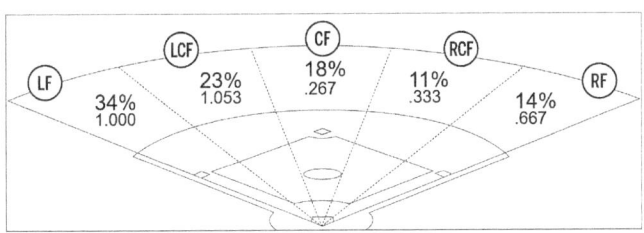

Strike Zone vs LHP   Strike Zone vs RHP

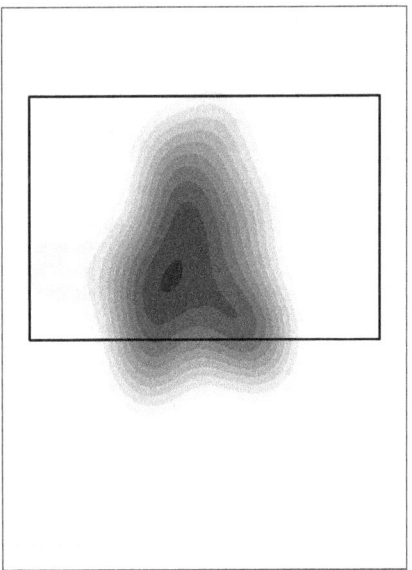

Type	Frequency	Velocity	H Movement	V Movement
● Fastball	100.0%	78.2 [54]	-9.2 [88]	-31.5 [54]

Keston Hiura   2B

Born: 08/02/96   Age: 24   Bats: R   Throws: R
Height: 6'0"   Weight: 202   Origin: Round 1, 2017 Draft (#9 overall)

YEAR	TEAM	LVL	AGE	PA	R	2B	3B	HR	RBI	BB	K	SB	CS	AVG/OBP/SLG
2018	CAR	HI-A	21	228	38	16	3	7	23	14	47	4	6	.320/.382/.529
2018	BLX	AA	21	307	36	18	2	6	20	22	56	11	5	.272/.339/.416
2019	SA	AAA	22	243	44	16	1	19	46	23	64	7	2	.329/.407/.681
2019	MIL	MLB	22	348	51	23	2	19	49	25	107	9	3	.303/.368/.570
2020	MIL	MLB	23	246	30	4	0	13	32	16	85	3	2	.212/.297/.410
2021 FS	MIL	MLB	24	600	79	24	3	25	86	40	197	7	3	.236/.308/.432
2021 DC	MIL	MLB	24	599	78	24	3	25	85	40	196	7	3	.236/.308/.432

Comparables: Mark Reynolds, Paul DeJong, Pedro Álvarez

It seemed reasonable, given Hiura's amateur and minor-league track record, to hope that his high rookie strikeout rate would be resolved by simple adjustments. A (shortened) season later, it's clear that more than tweaks and a moment to catch his breath will be required. Beaten consistently by high fastballs, Hiura has shown no facility for a shortened or secondary swing. Pitchers are able to exploit him as a result. He's clearly not going to add value as a defender, so going forward, his utility will depend on finding a more flexible approach and a more fluid set of mechanics in the box.

YEAR	TEAM	LVL	AGE	PA	DRC+	BABIP	BRR	FRAA	WARP
2018	CAR	HI-A	21	228	158	.386	0.6	2B(15): 0.6	1.5
2018	BLX	AA	21	307	116	.323	0.6	2B(64): -3.5	0.5
2019	SA	AAA	22	243	154	.389	0.0	2B(46): -1.6	2.1
2019	MIL	MLB	22	348	114	.402	-0.5	2B(81): -4.9	1.3
2020	MIL	MLB	23	246	97	.273	-0.2	2B(49): -5.6	0.0
2021 FS	MIL	MLB	24	600	101	.320	0.2	2B 0	1.9
2021 DC	MIL	MLB	24	599	101	.320	0.2	1B 0, 2B 0	1.1

Keston Hiura, continued

Batted Ball Distribution

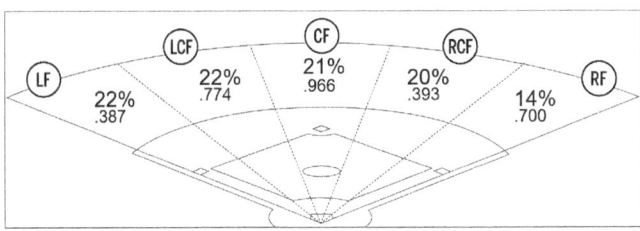

Strike Zone vs LHP   Strike Zone vs RHP

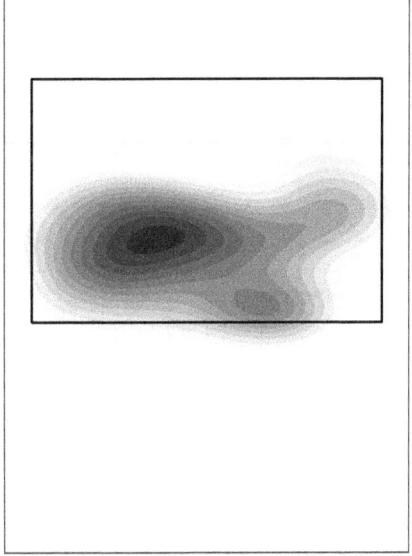

Milwaukee Brewers 2021

Tim Lopes 2B

Born: 06/24/94   Age: 27   Bats: R   Throws: R
Height: 5'11"   Weight: 180   Origin: Round 6, 2012 Draft (#191 overall)

YEAR	TEAM	LVL	AGE	PA	R	2B	3B	HR	RBI	BB	K	SB	CS	AVG/OBP/SLG
2018	BUF	AAA	24	385	41	19	3	2	29	26	58	18	8	.277/.325/.364
2019	TAC	AAA	25	420	59	31	2	10	60	36	72	26	9	.302/.362/.476
2019	SEA	MLB	25	128	11	7	0	1	12	15	29	6	3	.270/.359/.360
2020	SEA	MLB	26	151	16	12	0	2	15	6	34	5	0	.238/.278/.364
2021 FS	MIL	MLB	27	600	65	26	2	10	63	44	140	13	4	.238/.300/.353
2021 DC	MIL	MLB	27	230	25	10	0	4	24	17	53	4	2	.238/.300/.353

Comparables: Mark Smith, Larry Bigbie, Tony Longmire

In a Mariners organization bursting with players who are just very, very excited for the opportunity, Lopes is perhaps their patron saint. He demonstrates no skills one would consider above-average for a major leaguer, and it's perfectly in keeping with his profile that his 2020 DRA (93) was better than his 2020 DRC+. Nonetheless, Lopes is one of those players bound to stick around the big leagues far longer than his skillset warrants, the Henry Cotto of our wearying times. Expect him to bounce around the outer rims of the MLB galaxy before inexplicably hitting a home run in an ALCS game and achieving folk hero status. Best guess here says it's for the Yankees. For now, he'll have to settle for playing for the Brewers following a December waiver claim.

YEAR	TEAM	LVL	AGE	PA	DRC+	BABIP	BRR	FRAA	WARP
2018	BUF	AAA	24	385	107	.322	6.9	2B(69): 4.4, 3B(18): -1.0, LF(1): -0.1	1.9
2019	TAC	AAA	25	420	98	.344	2.8	2B(63): -7.6, 3B(21): 0.8	0.9
2019	SEA	MLB	25	128	90	.354	0.2	LF(33): -0.2, 2B(3): 0.0, RF(3): -0.4	0.2
2020	SEA	MLB	26	151	81	.299	0.4	LF(17): -1.8, RF(12): 0.5, 3B(1): 0.0	-0.1
2021 FS	MIL	MLB	27	600	81	.300	0.5	3B 1, RF 1	0.3
2021 DC	MIL	MLB	27	230	81	.300	0.2	3B 0, RF 0	0.0

Tim Lopes, continued

Batted Ball Distribution

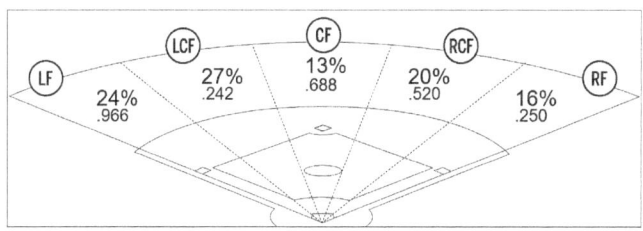

Strike Zone vs LHP   Strike Zone vs RHP

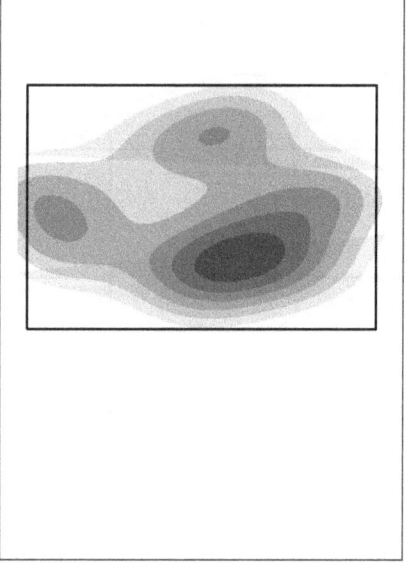

Type	Frequency	Velocity	H Movement	V Movement
● Fastball	100.0%	53.1 [-26]	-4.6 [110]	-74.9 [-68]

Brewers Player Analysis - 27

Milwaukee Brewers 2021

Mark Mathias 2B

Born: 08/02/94   Age: 26   Bats: R   Throws: R
Height: 6'0"   Weight: 200   Origin: Round 3, 2015 Draft (#93 overall)

YEAR	TEAM	LVL	AGE	PA	R	2B	3B	HR	RBI	BB	K	SB	CS	AVG/OBP/SLG
2018	AKR	AA	23	476	65	25	3	8	45	59	94	11	2	.232/.338/.370
2019	COL	AAA	24	478	62	31	2	12	59	51	91	13	2	.269/.355/.442
2020	MIL	MLB	25	36	2	3	0	0	4	0	7	1	0	.278/.278/.361
2021 FS	MIL	MLB	26	600	67	24	1	15	68	52	149	0	1	.217/.298/.353
2021 DC	MIL	MLB	26	65	7	2	0	1	7	5	16	0	0	.217/.298/.353

Comparables: Tug Hulett, Nick Franklin, Ian Kinsler

Middling. Mediocre. Milquetoast. Maybe Mathias deserves better than the connotations that go with those words, but they fit, both alliteratively and factually.

YEAR	TEAM	LVL	AGE	PA	DRC+	BABIP	BRR	FRAA	WARP
2018	AKR	AA	23	476	103	.277	-1.0	2B(105): 6.5, 1B(1): 0.0	1.3
2019	COL	AAA	24	478	104	.314	1.7	2B(52): 1.7, 3B(47): -1.8, SS(3): -0.7	1.8
2020	MIL	MLB	25	36	83	.345	-0.4	RF(8): 0.6, LF(4): 0.1, 1B(1): 0.1	0.0
2021 FS	MIL	MLB	26	600	80	.271	-0.7	3B -3, 1B 2	0.0
2021 DC	MIL	MLB	26	65	80	.271	-0.1	3B 0, 1B 0	-0.1

Mark Mathias, continued

Batted Ball Distribution

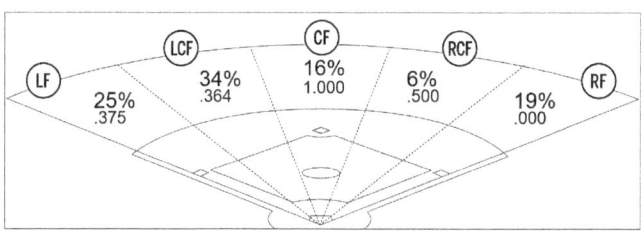

Strike Zone vs LHP   Strike Zone vs RHP

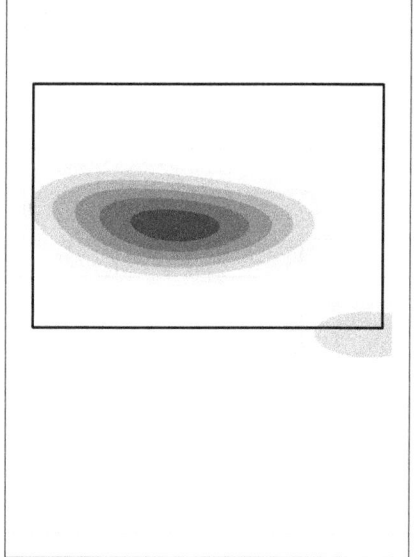

Omar Narváez C

Born: 02/10/92   Age: 29   Bats: L   Throws: R
Height: 5'11"   Weight: 220   Origin: International Free Agent, 2008

YEAR	TEAM	LVL	AGE	PA	R	2B	3B	HR	RBI	BB	K	SB	CS	AVG/OBP/SLG
2018	CHW	MLB	26	322	30	14	1	9	30	38	65	0	2	.275/.366/.429
2019	SEA	MLB	27	482	63	12	0	22	55	47	92	0	0	.278/.353/.460
2020	MIL	MLB	28	126	8	4	0	2	10	16	39	0	0	.176/.294/.269
2021 FS	MIL	MLB	29	600	73	22	1	18	75	68	139	0	1	.243/.335/.394
2021 DC	MIL	MLB	29	299	36	11	0	9	37	33	69	0	0	.243/.335/.394

Comparables: Jim Pagliaroni, Tim Hosley, Russell Martin

In 2019, Narváez finished 31st (out of 33) in our holistic Catcher Defensive Adjustment. In 2020, this time out of 31, he finished first. First! What a happy turn of events, and exactly what he needed in order to go from disposable second-division starter (albeit one who hit .277/.362/.419 from 2017-19) to plausible All-Star Game participant. In a cruel twist of fate, Narváez's stick is what failed him last season. His bat speed stayed in quarantine, and he started striking out at an alarming rate, as well as generating much less authoritative contact when he did meet the ball. The good news: if you had to guess that only one of these transformations will stick in 2021, the better bet would be the defensive one. The bad news: it's still a gamble.

YEAR	TEAM	P. COUNT	FRM RUNS	BLK RUNS	THRW RUNS	TOT RUNS
2018	CHW	11337	-10.8	-4.6	-0.1	-15.6
2019	SEA	13812	-8.2	-4.3	-1.0	-13.5
2020	MIL	4886	4.2	0.1	0.1	4.4
2021	MIL	10822	-2.7	-3.3	-0.3	-6.3
2021	MIL	10822	-2.7	-1.2	-0.3	-4.2

YEAR	TEAM	LVL	AGE	PA	DRC+	BABIP	BRR	FRAA	WARP
2018	CHW	MLB	26	322	109	.330	0.0	C(85): -17.6	0.0
2019	SEA	MLB	27	482	123	.306	-1.5	C(98): -12.3, 2B(1): -0.0	2.3
2020	MIL	MLB	28	126	77	.254	-0.1	C(39): -0.4	0.3
2021 FS	MIL	MLB	29	600	99	.298	-0.9	C -10, 2B 0	1.3
2021 DC	MIL	MLB	29	299	99	.298	-0.4	C -7	0.5

Omar Narváez, continued

Batted Ball Distribution

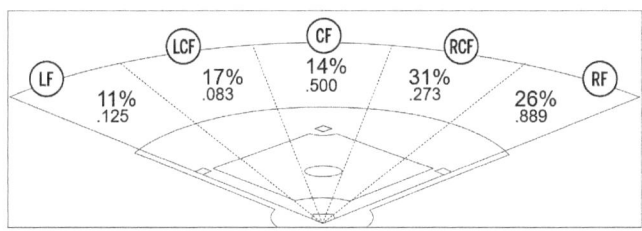

Strike Zone vs LHP   Strike Zone vs RHP

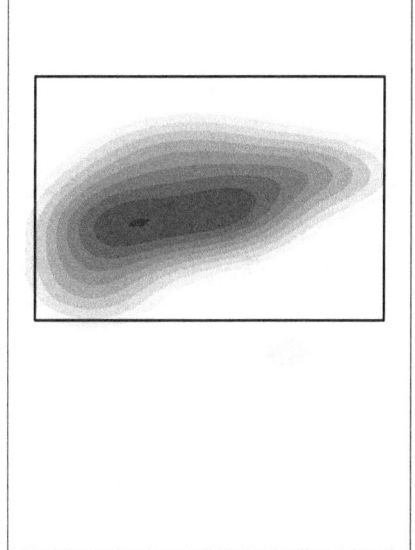

Milwaukee Brewers 2021

Jacob Nottingham   C

Born: 04/03/95   Age: 26   Bats: R   Throws: R
Height: 6'2"   Weight: 220   Origin: Round 6, 2013 Draft (#167 overall)

YEAR	TEAM	LVL	AGE	PA	R	2B	3B	HR	RBI	BB	K	SB	CS	AVG/OBP/SLG
2018	RMV	AAA	23	196	33	10	2	10	36	14	59	2	1	.281/.347/.528
2018	MIL	MLB	23	24	2	1	0	0	0	4	8	0	0	.200/.333/.250
2019	SA	AAA	24	332	40	21	0	5	40	28	95	6	1	.231/.313/.355
2019	MIL	MLB	24	7	1	0	0	1	4	0	2	0	0	.333/.429/.833
2020	MIL	MLB	25	54	8	1	0	4	13	5	20	0	0	.188/.278/.458
2021 FS	MIL	MLB	26	600	70	24	1	19	68	44	203	1	1	.207/.285/.368
2021 DC	MIL	MLB	26	153	18	6	0	5	17	11	52	0	0	.207/.285/.368

Comparables: Max Ramirez, Josh Donaldson, Tyler Flowers

Even the meanest foul tip to the mask won't leave one as reliably whiplashed or confused as trying to pin down Nottingham's ever-moving reputation as a prospect. Initially, he was a bat-first catcher, unlikely even to stick at that spot. Then, he and Brewers field coordinator and catching instructor Charlie Greene worked tirelessly together until he emerged as a solid defender—but suddenly, one without adequate punch. Now, there's some evidence that he's finding the (modestly) happy medium, He still has swing-and-miss issues at the plate and occasional lapses behind it, but he projects as a solid backup with positive tactical value.

YEAR	TEAM	P. COUNT	FRM RUNS	BLK RUNS	THRW RUNS	TOT RUNS
2018	MIL	955	-0.7	0.2	0.0	-0.5
2018	RMV	4222	1.5	-1.1	-0.2	0.2
2019	MIL	163	0.0	-0.1		-0.1
2019	SA	9444	12.0	0.0	-0.9	11.1
2020	MIL	2326	1.6	0.0	0.0	1.6
2021	MIL	4810	0.6	0.9	0.2	1.7
2021	MIL	4810	0.6	1.0	0.2	1.8

YEAR	TEAM	LVL	AGE	PA	DRC+	BABIP	BRR	FRAA	WARP
2018	RMV	AAA	23	196	95	.367	-0.6	C(32): -0.3, 1B(9): -0.0	0.3
2018	MIL	MLB	23	24	71	.333	-0.1	C(8): -0.5	0.0
2019	SA	AAA	24	332	73	.318	-1.4	C(66): 11.7, 1B(8): 0.2	1.4
2019	MIL	MLB	24	7	96	.333		C(6): -0.3, 1B(1): -0.0	0.0
2020	MIL	MLB	25	54	82	.208	0.0	C(19): 0.7	0.4
2021 FS	MIL	MLB	26	600	78	.289	-0.8	C 6, 1B 1	1.2
2021 DC	MIL	MLB	26	153	78	.289	-0.2	C 2, 1B 0	0.3

Jacob Nottingham, continued

Batted Ball Distribution

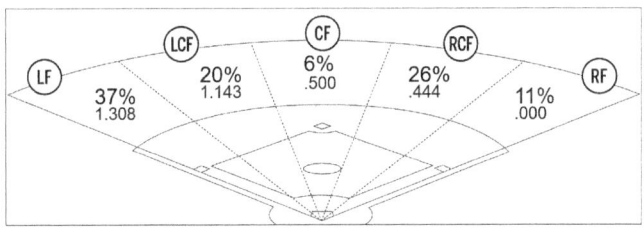

Strike Zone vs LHP   ### Strike Zone vs RHP

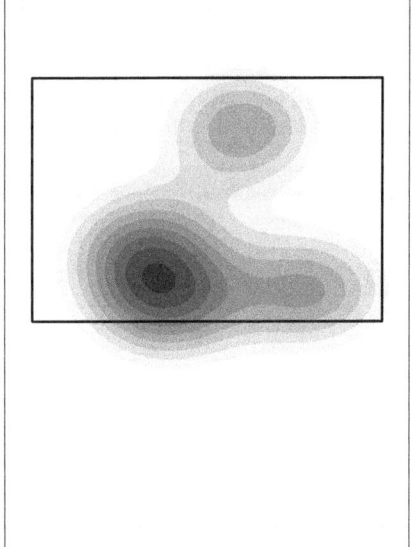

Manny Piña C

Born: 06/05/87 Age: 34 Bats: R Throws: R
Height: 6'0" Weight: 222 Origin: International Free Agent, 2004

YEAR	TEAM	LVL	AGE	PA	R	2B	3B	HR	RBI	BB	K	SB	CS	AVG/OBP/SLG
2018	MIL	MLB	31	337	39	13	2	9	28	21	62	2	0	.252/.307/.395
2019	MIL	MLB	32	179	10	8	0	7	25	16	50	0	0	.228/.313/.411
2020	MIL	MLB	33	45	4	1	0	2	5	3	11	0	0	.231/.333/.410
2021 FS	MIL	MLB	34	600	70	21	1	20	77	43	146	2	1	.232/.304/.390
2021 DC	MIL	MLB	34	166	19	5	0	5	21	12	40	0	1	.232/.304/.390

Comparables: Adam Melhuse, Damian Miller, John Buck

It seems lazy to compare Piña to a pineapple itself. He's stout, is tough and (in certain situations, given certain vulnerabilities) can deliver a jolt of unexpected pain in a couple of ways. He adds a bit of levity and passion to a clubhouse, does the dirty work required of a backup catcher with aplomb and has a balanced skill set on the field. He has to be used wisely to be valuable (keep pineapple off your pizzas, people!), but he's nice to have around. Plus, he too appeared in the background of every episode of *Psych*. (He didn't, but be honest: you wouldn't have known either way.)

YEAR	TEAM	P. COUNT	FRM RUNS	BLK RUNS	THRW RUNS	TOT RUNS
2018	MIL	12539	4.8	1.3	0.5	6.7
2019	MIL	6204	6.4	2.0	-0.1	8.3
2020	MIL	1750	1.0	0.1	-0.1	1.0
2021	MIL	6012	0.0	0.3	0.7	1.0
2021	MIL	6012	0.0	0.5	0.7	1.2

YEAR	TEAM	LVL	AGE	PA	DRC+	BABIP	BRR	FRAA	WARP
2018	MIL	MLB	31	337	90	.285	-3.6	C(92): 7.0, 1B(1): -0.0	1.6
2019	MIL	MLB	32	179	89	.284	-0.5	C(53): 8.3, 3B(1): -0.0	1.4
2020	MIL	MLB	33	45	100	.269	-0.2	C(13): 0.4	0.3
2021 FS	MIL	MLB	34	600	89	.280	-0.7	C 3, 1B 0	1.9
2021 DC	MIL	MLB	34	166	89	.280	-0.2	C 1	0.5

Manny Piña, continued

Batted Ball Distribution

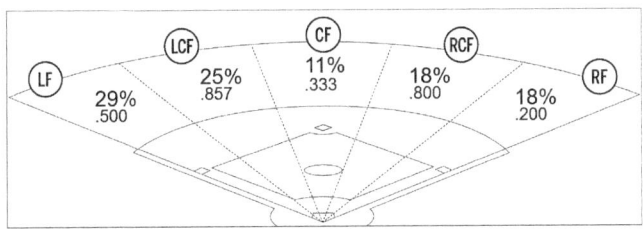

Strike Zone vs LHP

Strike Zone vs RHP

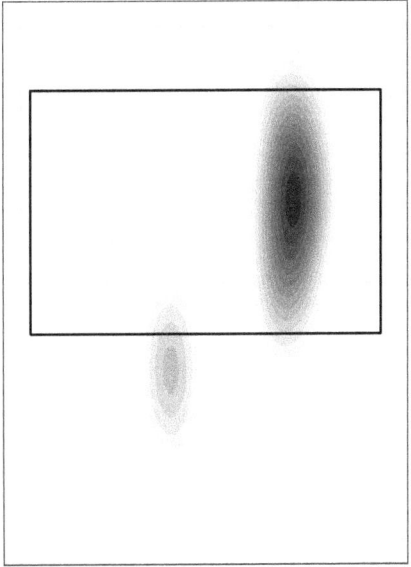

Tyrone Taylor CF

Born: 01/22/94 Age: 27 Bats: R Throws: R
Height: 6'0" Weight: 194 Origin: Round 2, 2012 Draft (#92 overall)

YEAR	TEAM	LVL	AGE	PA	R	2B	3B	HR	RBI	BB	K	SB	CS	AVG/OBP/SLG
2018	RMV	AAA	24	481	73	23	9	20	80	27	74	13	4	.278/.321/.504
2019	SA	AAA	25	375	44	20	1	14	59	28	85	5	0	.269/.334/.461
2019	MIL	MLB	25	12	1	2	0	0	1	1	1	0	0	.400/.500/.600
2020	MIL	MLB	26	41	6	4	0	2	6	2	8	0	0	.237/.293/.500
2021 FS	MIL	MLB	27	600	71	24	2	23	78	37	129	2	1	.240/.299/.418
2021 DC	MIL	MLB	27	64	7	2	0	2	8	4	13	0	0	.240/.299/.418

Comparables: Scott Cousins, Cole Garner, Carlos Moncrief

Taylor has great speed, and his compact frame and torque-heavy swing imply real power potential. He's also a solid if unspectacular defensive outfielder. Unfortunately, he still hasn't found consistent success at the upper levels, or in the big leagues. His swing is the thing: he has a complicated load, in which his hands come way down and his barrel tips a bit, and he doesn't seem able to get loft on his swing and deliver the barrel to the hitting zone on time as consistently as he might. Unless that changes, he'll be confined to a fourth-outfielder role. There are worse fates.

YEAR	TEAM	LVL	AGE	PA	DRC+	BABIP	BRR	FRAA	WARP
2018	RMV	AAA	24	481	98	.292	2.3	CF(56): 0.5, LF(39): 7.2, RF(26): 1.0	1.8
2019	SA	AAA	25	375	92	.317	0.3	RF(47): 1.6, CF(43): 8.5, LF(5): 0.2	1.7
2019	MIL	MLB	25	12	88	.444	-0.4	RF(8): -0.1, CF(3): -0.3	0.0
2020	MIL	MLB	26	41	103	.250	-0.5	RF(10): -0.3, CF(9): -0.3, LF(2): -0.0	0.0
2021 FS	MIL	MLB	27	600	93	.273	-0.5	RF 3, LF 0	1.4
2021 DC	MIL	MLB	27	64	93	.273	-0.1	RF 0	0.1

Tyrone Taylor, continued

Batted Ball Distribution

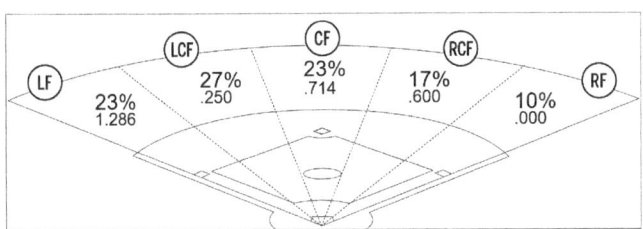

Strike Zone vs LHP   Strike Zone vs RHP

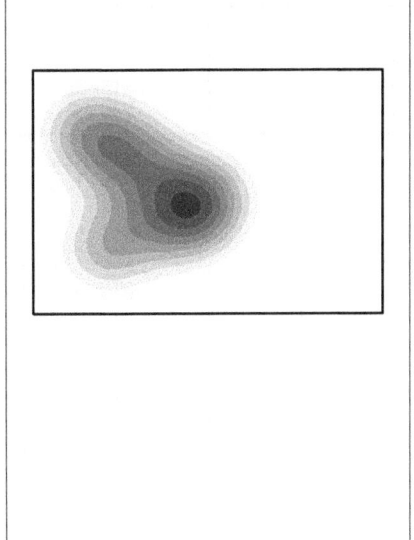

Milwaukee Brewers 2021

Luis Urías 2B

Born: 06/03/97 Age: 24 Bats: R Throws: R
Height: 5'9" Weight: 186 Origin: International Free Agent, 2013

YEAR	TEAM	LVL	AGE	PA	R	2B	3B	HR	RBI	BB	K	SB	CS	AVG/OBP/SLG
2018	ELP	AAA	21	533	83	30	7	8	45	67	109	2	1	.296/.398/.447
2018	SD	MLB	21	53	5	1	0	2	5	3	10	1	0	.208/.264/.354
2019	ELP	AAA	22	339	62	19	4	19	50	36	62	7	2	.315/.398/.600
2019	SD	MLB	22	249	27	8	1	4	24	25	56	0	1	.223/.329/.326
2020	MIL	MLB	23	120	11	4	1	0	11	10	32	2	2	.239/.308/.294
2021 FS	MIL	MLB	24	600	72	23	2	13	66	62	132	1	1	.246/.340/.381
2021 DC	MIL	MLB	24	491	59	19	2	11	54	51	108	0	1	.246/.340/.381

Comparables: Dansby Swanson, Billy Consolo, Gene Alley

Calling 2020 a lost season for Urías might be too charitable. His athleticism and his feel to hit continued a two-year downward trend. No unexpected power showed up, and although some tweaks to his swing suggest he's searching for some, there's no real evidence that it's coming. Acquired as potentially a long-term, dynamic shortstop, he needs to fix mechanical and approach problems just to make his way back to being a solid everyday player. Even then, it might not be at short, after all.

YEAR	TEAM	LVL	AGE	PA	DRC+	BABIP	BRR	FRAA	WARP
2018	ELP	AAA	21	533	116	.373	1.4	2B(90): 10.2, SS(20): 3.4, 3B(11): 1.1	3.7
2018	SD	MLB	21	53	84	.216	0.3	2B(12): -0.2	0.1
2019	ELP	AAA	22	339	124	.343	2.5	SS(53): 8.5, 2B(21): 4.1	3.8
2019	SD	MLB	22	249	83	.284	0.0	SS(41): -5.4, 2B(26): -1.7, 3B(1): -0.2	-0.2
2020	MIL	MLB	23	120	64	.338	-0.6	3B(30): 2.0, 2B(10): 1.7, SS(8): 0.4	0.0
2021 FS	MIL	MLB	24	600	103	.304	-0.6	3B 5, SS 0	2.4
2021 DC	MIL	MLB	24	491	103	.304	-0.5	3B 4, SS 0	1.5

Luis Urías, continued

Batted Ball Distribution

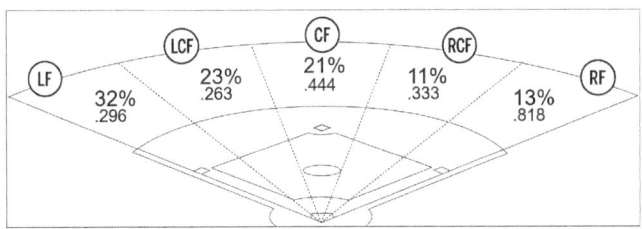

Strike Zone vs LHP

Strike Zone vs RHP

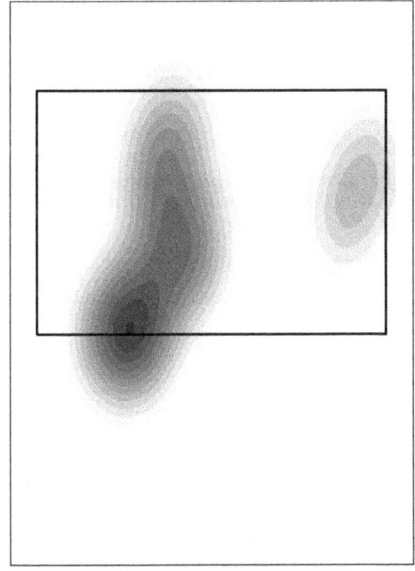
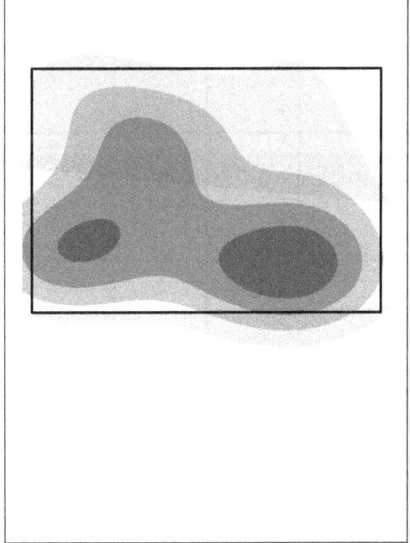

Kolten Wong 2B

Born: 10/10/90 Age: 30 Bats: L Throws: R
Height: 5'7" Weight: 185 Origin: Round 1, 2011 Draft (#22 overall)

YEAR	TEAM	LVL	AGE	PA	R	2B	3B	HR	RBI	BB	K	SB	CS	AVG/OBP/SLG
2018	STL	MLB	27	407	41	18	2	9	38	31	60	6	5	.249/.332/.388
2019	STL	MLB	28	549	61	25	4	11	59	47	83	24	4	.285/.361/.423
2020	STL	MLB	29	208	26	4	2	1	16	20	30	5	2	.265/.350/.326
2021 FS	MIL	MLB	30	600	82	27	4	13	60	54	101	14	5	.259/.347/.406
2021 DC	MIL	MLB	30	614	84	28	4	13	61	55	103	14	5	.259/.347/.406

Comparables: Ray Durham, D'Angelo Jimenez, Mark Ellis

Does it make sense to describe a player as both steady and volatile? You can make book on Wong providing speed, Gold Glove-caliber fielding, plenty of contact and enough walks to keep him from ever being a true lineup sink, but the quality of that contact careens wildly from year to year. In his good years Wong produces just enough pop to be an above-average bat at the keystone, but more frequently he's the Midwest's premiere supplier of routine grounders. Last year Wong put up one of the league's lowest barrel percentages and posted the worst isolated power mark in Missouri, a state where Nicky Lopez is also employed. His ever-present glove, wheels and on-base skills make him a nice complementary piece in the seven hole, but he'll usually break your heart if you cast Wong as a top-of-the-order spark plug. The Cardinals, who declined his affordable club option to begin the offseason, reinforced as much.

YEAR	TEAM	LVL	AGE	PA	DRC+	BABIP	BRR	FRAA	WARP
2018	STL	MLB	27	407	90	.275	-2.0	2B(119): 6.0	1.2
2019	STL	MLB	28	549	102	.321	3.2	2B(147): 18.6	4.1
2020	STL	MLB	29	208	86	.311	1.3	2B(53): 10.7	1.5
2021 FS	MIL	MLB	30	600	106	.299	0.9	2B 6	3.0
2021 DC	MIL	MLB	30	614	106	.299	0.9	2B 6	3.0

Kolten Wong, continued

Batted Ball Distribution

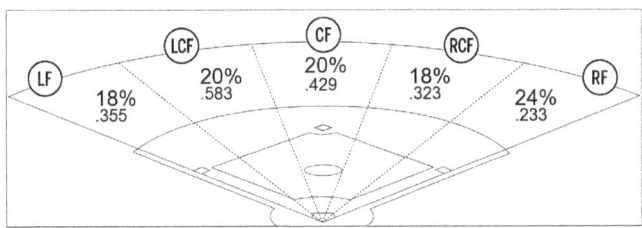

Strike Zone vs LHP   Strike Zone vs RHP

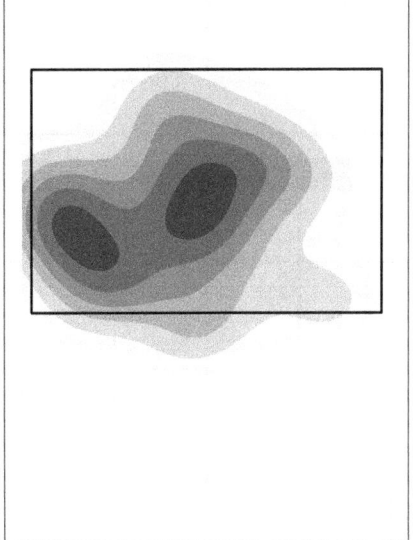

Christian Yelich RF

Born: 12/05/91 Age: 29 Bats: L Throws: R
Height: 6'3" Weight: 195 Origin: Round 1, 2010 Draft (#23 overall)

YEAR	TEAM	LVL	AGE	PA	R	2B	3B	HR	RBI	BB	K	SB	CS	AVG/OBP/SLG
2018	MIL	MLB	26	651	118	34	7	36	110	68	135	22	4	.326/.402/.598
2019	MIL	MLB	27	580	100	29	3	44	97	80	118	30	2	.329/.429/.671
2020	MIL	MLB	28	247	39	7	1	12	22	46	76	4	2	.205/.356/.430
2021 FS	MIL	MLB	29	600	95	25	2	30	89	84	163	16	4	.261/.373/.501
2021 DC	MIL	MLB	29	616	98	26	2	31	91	86	167	16	4	.261/.373/.501

Comparables: Nolan Reimold, Greg Vaughn, Mike Young

If there's any player whose 2020 demands to be ignored, it would seem to be Yelich. He still hit the ball harder on average than almost anyone in baseball, and he still drew tons of walks. Most of his numbers can be explained away as bad luck in a shortened season, and for a prime-aged, MVP-caliber player with a broad skill set, that sort of dismissal seems to be in order. And yet...Yelich's swing was never quite right: he lost the ability to consistently generate loft; he whiffed on high, inside fastballs and low, outside breaking balls not only more often than he has in the past but at a truly disastrous rate; and he was slower on the bases and lousy in left field. It's easy to call it a lost season after a bifurcated spring training and with endless externalities dividing everyone's attention; it just doesn't quite explain this. Since Yelich will turn 30 in December, an explanation would be a big comfort.

YEAR	TEAM	LVL	AGE	PA	DRC+	BABIP	BRR	FRAA	WARP
2018	MIL	MLB	26	651	143	.373	2.4	LF(90): -7.3, RF(75): 2.1, CF(20): 0.4	4.8
2019	MIL	MLB	27	580	166	.355	3.7	RF(124): -1.6, LF(6): 0.5, CF(1): -0.0	6.5
2020	MIL	MLB	28	247	107	.259	0.2	LF(51): -7.4	-0.1
2021 FS	MIL	MLB	29	600	135	.326	0.7	LF -5, CF 0	3.6
2021 DC	MIL	MLB	29	616	135	.326	0.7	LF -5	3.9

Christian Yelich, continued

Batted Ball Distribution

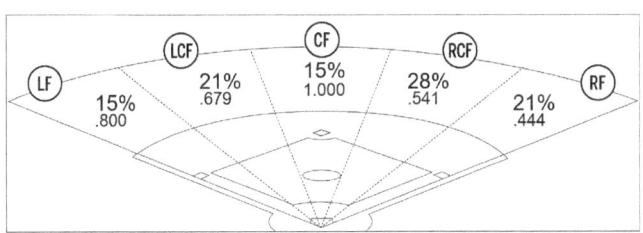

Strike Zone vs LHP   Strike Zone vs RHP

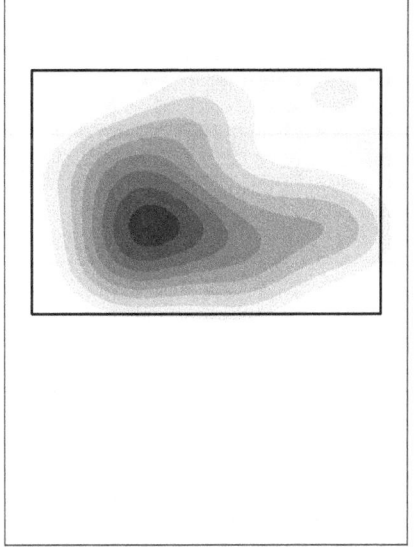

Brewers Player Analysis - 43

Brett Anderson   LHP

Born: 02/01/88   Age: 33   Bats: L   Throws: L
Height: 6'4"   Weight: 230   Origin: Round 2, 2006 Draft (#55 overall)

YEAR	TEAM	LVL	AGE	W	L	SV	G	GS	IP	H	HR	BB/9	K/9	K	GB%	BABIP
2018	NAS	AAA	30	2	1	0	7	7	32^1	32	0	1.7	10.0	36	57.3%	.340
2018	OAK	MLB	30	4	5	0	17	17	80^1	90	10	1.5	5.3	47	55.4%	.309
2019	OAK	MLB	31	13	9	0	31	31	176	181	20	2.5	4.6	90	54.0%	.280
2020	MIL	MLB	32	4	4	0	10	10	47	50	6	1.9	6.1	32	59.6%	.293
2021 FS	MIL	MLB	33	9	8	0	26	26	150	158	20	2.7	6.1	101	56.1%	.291
2021 DC	MIL	MLB	33	4	4	0	16	16	76	80	10	2.7	6.1	51	56.1%	.291

Comparables: Trevor Cahill, Jhoulys Chacín, Homer Bailey

Whenever Anderson pitches, you kind of wish you could just call it off and spare everyone the aggravation. He needs a good-sized zone, so if he's not getting calls early, tensions rise quickly between his team and the umpires. Hitters, meanwhile, spike a lot of helmets in regret just beyond first base as they try to tee off on a five-pitch assortment of borderline strikes that dive past their sweet spot, leading to weak groundouts. Then, finally, the lack of strikeouts catches up to Anderson, as a ball trickles through or finds a gap with runners aboard, and the southpaw stomps to the showers, muttering about the shift or modern pitcher usage or his crummy luck. It's no fun, but it keeps working just well enough that no one wants to say "uncle."

YEAR	TEAM	LVL	AGE	WHIP	ERA	DRA-	WARP	MPH	FB%	WHF	CSP
2018	NAS	AAA	30	1.18	2.78	70	0.8				
2018	OAK	MLB	30	1.28	4.48	88	1.2	92.6	49.6%	17.1%	
2019	OAK	MLB	31	1.31	3.89	115	0.2	93.2	62.2%	17.1%	
2020	MIL	MLB	32	1.28	4.21	99	0.4	92.0	54.3%	19.7%	
2021 FS	MIL	MLB	33	1.35	4.33	100	1.4	92.8	58.4%	17.8%	49.7%
2021 DC	MIL	MLB	33	1.35	4.33	100	0.7	92.8	58.4%	17.8%	49.7%

Brett Anderson, continued

Pitch Shape vs LHH

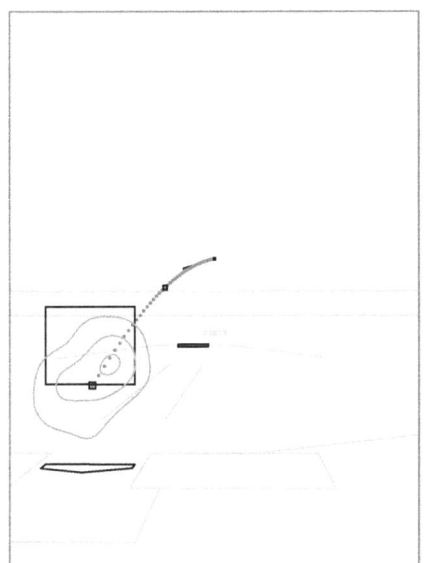

Pitch Shape vs RHH

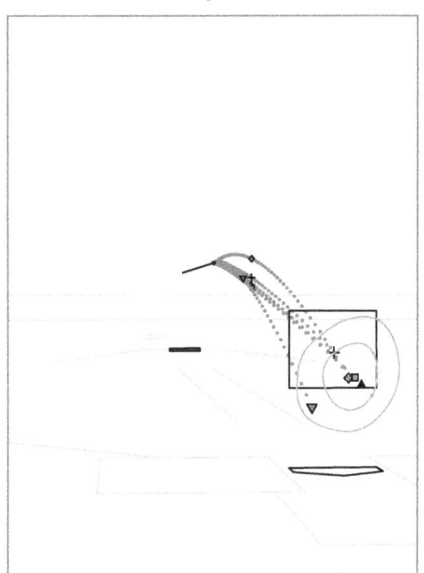

Type	Frequency	Velocity	H Movement	V Movement
● Fastball	3.2%	89.9 [92]	7.6 [96]	-16.2 [97]
□ Sinker	40.0%	90 [87]	13.2 [99]	-20.4 [100]
+ Cutter	11.0%	87.5 [95]	1.1 [80]	-21.6 [110]
▲ Changeup	24.1%	83 [91]	12.4 [96]	-27.1 [101]
▽ Slider	11.7%	82.3 [93]	-2.3 [89]	-40.9 [79]
◇ Curveball	10.0%	76.2 [90]	-6.3 [95]	-54.3 [87]

Corbin Burnes   RHP

Born: 10/22/94   Age: 26   Bats: R   Throws: R
Height: 6'3"   Weight: 225   Origin: Round 4, 2016 Draft (#111 overall)

YEAR	TEAM	LVL	AGE	W	L	SV	G	GS	IP	H	HR	BB/9	K/9	K	GB%	BABIP
2018	RMV	AAA	23	3	4	0	19	13	78^2	83	7	3.5	9.3	81	46.9%	.347
2018	MIL	MLB	23	7	0	1	30	0	38	27	4	2.6	8.3	35	48.5%	.235
2019	SA	AAA	24	0	1	0	8	7	22^1	29	2	3.6	10.1	25	48.5%	.409
2019	MIL	MLB	24	1	5	1	32	4	49	70	17	3.7	12.9	70	44.1%	.424
2020	MIL	MLB	25	4	1	0	12	9	59^2	37	2	3.6	13.3	88	47.2%	.285
2021 FS	MIL	MLB	26	10	7	0	26	26	150	124	19	4.0	11.5	191	45.9%	.298
2021 DC	MIL	MLB	26	9	7	0	27	27	137.7	114	17	4.0	11.5	175	45.9%	.298

Comparables: Michael Feliz, John Gant, Ryan Helsley

Home-run rates tend to even out from one season to the next, but if you even begin to read Burnes' breakout campaign as merely the good kind of regression, you'll miss out on a much richer, better and truer story. Blessed with a live arm that allows him to generate both velocity and spin, Burnes saw too many of his pitches flatten out and fly straight down the middle in 2019. He and the Brewers went to work before the season even ended, with bullpen coach Steve Karsay encouraging him as he took his first steps toward fixing his issues. Together, Burnes and the organization got him back to throwing a sinker, rather than a four-seamer, and he developed a truly filthy cutter. His 2020 was even more truncated than most, but he's found a pair of pitches with which he can miss bats, manage contact and throw enough strikes to keep hitters hacking.

YEAR	TEAM	LVL	AGE	WHIP	ERA	DRA-	WARP	MPH	FB%	WHF	CSP
2018	RMV	AAA	23	1.45	5.15	75	1.8				
2018	MIL	MLB	23	1.00	2.61	75	0.7	97.0	58.8%	32.0%	
2019	SA	AAA	24	1.70	8.46	76	0.6				
2019	MIL	MLB	24	1.84	8.82	102	0.3	97.7	56.8%	36.7%	
2020	MIL	MLB	25	1.02	2.11	60	1.8	97.5	67.7%	34.8%	
2021 FS	MIL	MLB	26	1.28	3.64	84	2.8	97.5	63.2%	35.1%	43.4%
2021 DC	MIL	MLB	26	1.28	3.64	84	2.3	97.5	63.2%	35.1%	43.4%

Corbin Burnes, continued

Pitch Shape vs LHH

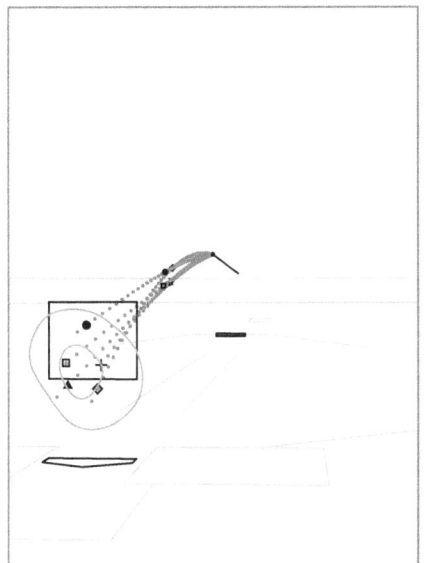

Pitch Shape vs RHH

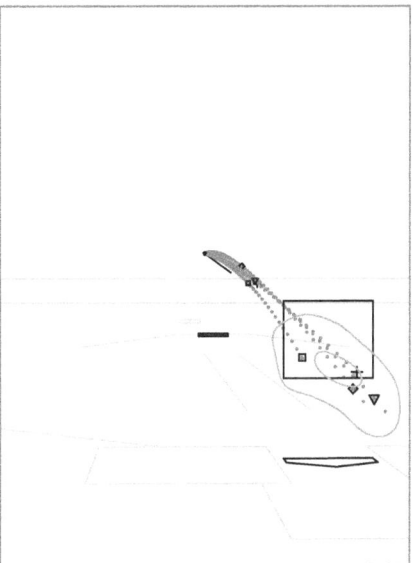

Type	Frequency	Velocity	H Movement	V Movement
● Fastball	7.1%	95.8 [110]	-2.5 [120]	-13.5 [105]
☐ Sinker	30.8%	96.2 [119]	-10.8 [117]	-15 [118]
+ Cutter	29.7%	93.1 [130]	3.9 [113]	-19.6 [118]
▲ Changeup	11.0%	89.1 [115]	-11.1 [103]	-24.8 [107]
▽ Slider	12.6%	86.7 [112]	7.1 [107]	-32.1 [105]
◇ Curveball	8.7%	81.3 [110]	9.8 [109]	-42.8 [113]

J.P. Feyereisen RHP

Born: 02/07/93   Age: 28   Bats: R   Throws: R
Height: 6'2"   Weight: 215   Origin: Round 16, 2014 Draft (#488 overall)

YEAR	TEAM	LVL	AGE	W	L	SV	G	GS	IP	H	HR	BB/9	K/9	K	GB%	BABIP
2018	SWB	AAA	25	6	6	1	37	0	60	56	5	3.8	8.8	59	33.1%	.321
2019	SWB	AAA	26	10	2	7	40	0	61^1	37	6	4.5	13.8	94	35.2%	.270
2020	MIL	MLB	27	0	0	0	6	0	9^1	4	3	4.8	6.8	7	33.3%	.048
2021 FS	MIL	MLB	28	2	2	0	57	0	50	44	8	4.4	10.6	59	36.2%	.293
2021 DC	MIL	MLB	28	2	2	0	42	0	38	34	6	4.4	10.6	45	36.2%	.293

Comparables: Rowan Wick, Jake Barrett, Justin Shafer

With mid-90s rising heat and a pair of pitches that play off it well, Feyereisen just has to throw strikes to be an excellent reliever. (Alas.)

YEAR	TEAM	LVL	AGE	WHIP	ERA	DRA-	WARP	MPH	FB%	WHF	CSP
2018	SWB	AAA	25	1.35	3.45	103	0.0				
2019	SWB	AAA	26	1.11	2.49	42	2.5				
2020	MIL	MLB	27	0.96	5.79	132	-0.1	94.6	54.0%	34.7%	
2021 FS	MIL	MLB	28	1.39	4.47	99	0.3	94.6	54.0%	34.7%	39.3%
2021 DC	MIL	MLB	28	1.39	4.47	99	0.2	94.6	54.0%	34.7%	39.3%

J.P. Feyereisen, continued

Pitch Shape vs LHH

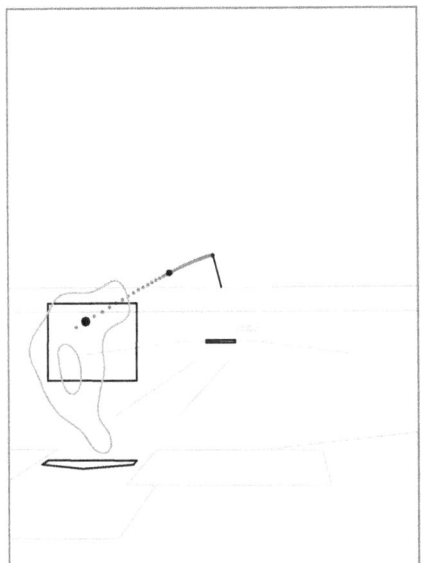

Pitch Shape vs RHH

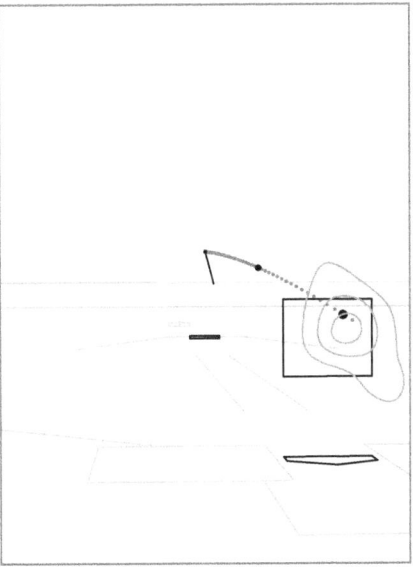

Type	Frequency	Velocity	H Movement	V Movement
● Fastball	54.0%	93.6 [103]	-4.4 [111]	-10.5 [113]
▲ Changeup	18.0%	87.7 [110]	-13.7 [89]	-28.9 [96]
▽ Slider	28.0%	84.3 [101]	6.5 [105]	-36.8 [91]

Milwaukee Brewers 2021

Josh Hader LHP

Born: 04/07/94 Age: 27 Bats: L Throws: L
Height: 6'3" Weight: 180 Origin: Round 19, 2012 Draft (#582 overall)

YEAR	TEAM	LVL	AGE	W	L	SV	G	GS	IP	H	HR	BB/9	K/9	K	GB%	BABIP
2018	MIL	MLB	24	6	1	12	55	0	81^1	36	9	3.3	15.8	143	28.0%	.221
2019	MIL	MLB	25	3	5	37	61	0	75^2	41	15	2.4	16.4	138	22.0%	.232
2020	MIL	MLB	26	1	2	13	21	0	19	8	3	4.7	14.7	31	26.5%	.161
2021 FS	MIL	MLB	27	3	2	33	57	0	50	32	6	4.1	14.4	80	30.0%	.280
2021 DC	MIL	MLB	27	2	2	33	55	0	57	37	7	4.1	14.4	91	30.0%	.280

Comparables: Edwin Díaz, Tyler Glasnow, José Leclerc

Maybe it's impossible to sustain the level of dominance and utility Hader achieved in 2018. What we can say for sure is that it's impossible to sustain without a third reliable pitch or plus command. Hader remains a strikeout monster, but after two years fanning nearly half his opposing batters, his K rate slipped under 40 percent. Believing his troublesome vulnerability to homers in 2019 stemmed from throwing too many fastballs, he upped his slider usage. That just made the plate elusive, so he developed a walk problem. To make matters worse, his velocity and whiff rate also dipped. Hader's average plate appearance lasted 4.8 pitches, which accelerated his move into a traditional closer role. He got at least four outs 72 times in the first two-and-a-half seasons of his career; in 2020, he did that once. He's firmly among the ranks of the one-inning relievers now, even if he's better than most of them.

YEAR	TEAM	LVL	AGE	WHIP	ERA	DRA-	WARP	MPH	FB%	WHF	CSP
2018	MIL	MLB	24	0.81	2.43	44	2.7	96.9	79.1%	39.4%	
2019	MIL	MLB	25	0.81	2.62	45	2.6	97.6	84.1%	41.7%	
2020	MIL	MLB	26	0.95	3.79	89	0.3	96.4	67.8%	38.7%	
2021 FS	MIL	MLB	27	1.12	2.83	67	1.2	97.1	78.9%	40.4%	49.6%
2021 DC	MIL	MLB	27	1.12	2.83	67	1.3	97.1	78.9%	40.4%	49.6%

Josh Hader, continued

Pitch Shape vs LHH

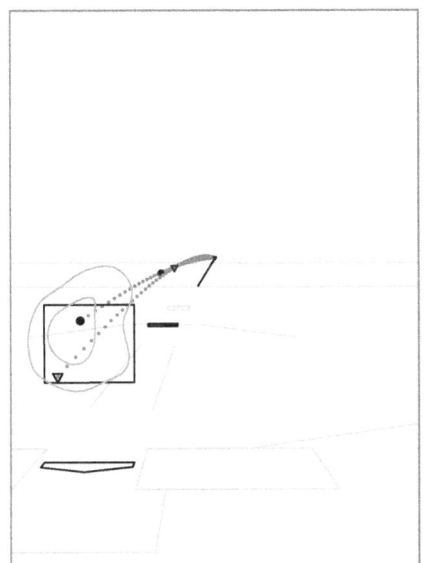

Pitch Shape vs RHH

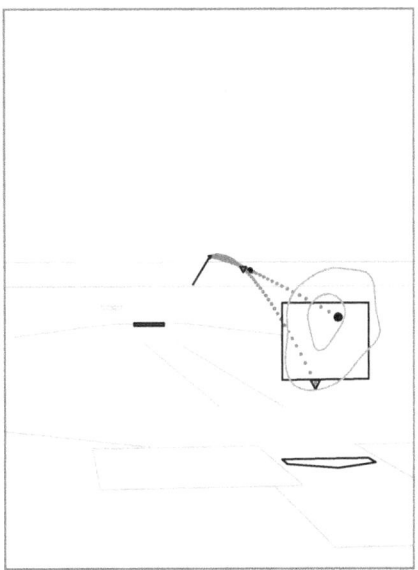

Type	Frequency	Velocity	H Movement	V Movement
● Fastball	67.5%	94.8 [107]	8.8 [90]	-12.1 [109]
▽ Slider	32.0%	80.5 [85]	-6.7 [105]	-38.1 [87]

Adrian Houser RHP

Born: 02/02/93 Age: 28 Bats: R Throws: R
Height: 6'3" Weight: 222 Origin: Round 2, 2011 Draft (#69 overall)

YEAR	TEAM	LVL	AGE	W	L	SV	G	GS	IP	H	HR	BB/9	K/9	K	GB%	BABIP
2018	BLX	AA	25	0	1	0	8	8	26²	30	3	2.4	10.1	30	48.1%	.370
2018	RMV	AAA	25	2	3	0	13	13	52	66	6	3.1	6.4	37	53.4%	.359
2018	MIL	MLB	25	0	0	0	7	0	13²	13	0	4.6	5.3	8	39.5%	.302
2019	SA	AAA	26	2	0	0	4	4	21¹	13	2	1.7	9.7	23	51.9%	.212
2019	MIL	MLB	26	6	7	0	35	18	111¹	101	14	3.0	9.5	117	53.8%	.304
2020	MIL	MLB	27	1	6	0	12	11	56	63	8	3.4	7.1	44	59.3%	.325
2021 FS	MIL	MLB	28	9	8	0	26	26	150	142	18	3.5	8.4	140	55.1%	.294
2021 DC	MIL	MLB	28	9	8	0	27	27	145.7	138	17	3.5	8.4	137	55.1%	.294

Comparables: Aaron Slegers, Austin Voth, John Gant

Unfortunately famous for repeatedly vomiting behind the mound when called upon in relief, Houser held down his lunch (or disposed of it in proper receptacles) as a full-time starter in 2020. On balance, he might be better off as a puking penman. His sinker is a good pitch, but not such an overwhelming one as to let him turn the lineup card over or pitch effectively to lefties with it, and his secondary stuff is pedestrian. His lousy ERA was no fluke. As a reliever, though, the stuff works, so maybe he just needs a manager willing to bring a bucket with them to the mound when they bring him in with runners on base.

YEAR	TEAM	LVL	AGE	WHIP	ERA	DRA-	WARP	MPH	FB%	WHF	CSP
2018	BLX	AA	25	1.39	4.72	94	0.3				
2018	RMV	AAA	25	1.62	5.19	97	0.6				
2018	MIL	MLB	25	1.46	3.29	112	0.0	96.1	66.4%	23.8%	
2019	SA	AAA	26	0.80	1.27	28	1.1				
2019	MIL	MLB	26	1.24	3.72	74	2.5	96.2	67.3%	24.3%	
2020	MIL	MLB	27	1.50	5.30	94	0.7	95.4	64.0%	22.5%	
2021 FS	MIL	MLB	28	1.34	4.07	93	2.0	95.9	65.9%	23.5%	46.1%
2021 DC	MIL	MLB	28	1.34	4.07	93	1.7	95.9	65.9%	23.5%	46.1%

Adrian Houser, continued

Pitch Shape vs LHH

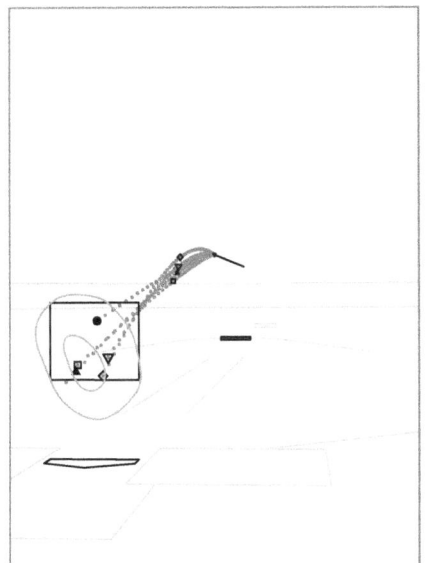

Pitch Shape vs RHH

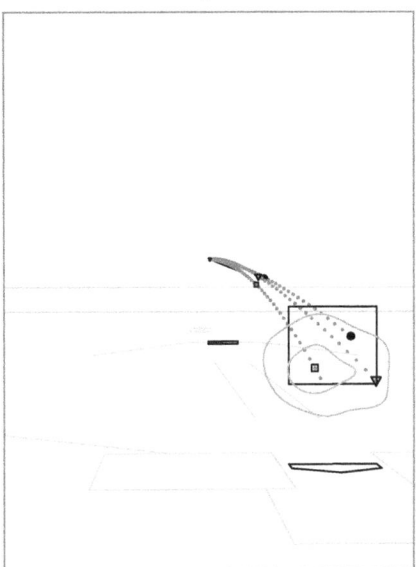

Type	Frequency	Velocity	H Movement	V Movement
● Fastball	20.4%	94 [105]	-6.2 [103]	-14 [103]
□ Sinker	43.6%	93.4 [105]	-13.6 [96]	-21.6 [97]
▲ Changeup	11.6%	85.1 [100]	-10.3 [107]	-29.2 [95]
▽ Slider	12.3%	85.8 [108]	4.6 [98]	-31.1 [108]
◇ Curveball	12.1%	80.7 [108]	4.3 [87]	-50.3 [96]

Eric Lauer   LHP

Born: 06/03/95   Age: 26   Bats: R   Throws: L
Height: 6'3"   Weight: 228   Origin: Round 1, 2016 Draft (#25 overall)

YEAR	TEAM	LVL	AGE	W	L	SV	G	GS	IP	H	HR	BB/9	K/9	K	GB%	BABIP
2018	LE	HI-A	23	0	0	0	1	1	3	3	0	3.0	12.0	4	50.0%	.500
2018	ELP	AAA	23	2	1	0	4	4	21¹	13	1	3.8	9.3	22	46.3%	.231
2018	SD	MLB	23	6	7	0	23	23	112	127	15	3.7	8.0	100	35.8%	.336
2019	SD	MLB	24	8	10	0	30	29	149²	158	20	3.1	8.3	138	40.5%	.318
2020	MIL	MLB	25	0	2	0	4	2	11	17	2	7.4	9.8	12	21.1%	.417
2021 FS	MIL	MLB	26	9	8	0	26	26	150	150	26	3.3	8.4	140	37.2%	.295
2021 DC	MIL	MLB	26	2	3	0	11	9	45.7	45	7	3.3	8.4	42	37.2%	.295

Comparables: Ryan Borucki, Conner Menez, Andrew Suárez

Things just didn't click for Lauer in the early stages of the shortened season, and the Brewers seized an opportunity to look beyond 2020. Lauer's release point was a bit down in his four appearances. His cutter flattened out, his slider bled into his cutter and his changeup was lifeless. Still, it was four total appearances, and Lauer has a track record to suggest he'd have recovered. Before he could, the team sent him to their alternate site and never brought him back, even as they got desperate for starting pitching down the stretch. Lauer will have to attempt a total reset in 2021, which figures to be difficult, but the Brewers seem to prefer having avoided allowing him to become Super Two-eligible to having given him a longer look.

YEAR	TEAM	LVL	AGE	WHIP	ERA	DRA-	WARP	MPH	FB%	WHF	CSP
2018	LE	HI-A	23	1.33	0.00	83	0.0				
2018	ELP	AAA	23	1.03	2.53	135	-0.2				
2018	SD	MLB	23	1.54	4.34	117	0.1	93.7	57.8%	20.6%	
2019	SD	MLB	24	1.40	4.45	99	1.5	94.1	53.0%	20.1%	
2020	MIL	MLB	25	2.36	13.09	162	-0.3	93.6	52.5%	29.1%	
2021 FS	MIL	MLB	26	1.36	4.59	103	1.2	93.9	54.1%	21.1%	50.9%
2021 DC	MIL	MLB	26	1.36	4.59	103	0.3	93.9	54.1%	21.1%	50.9%

Eric Lauer, continued

Pitch Shape vs LHH

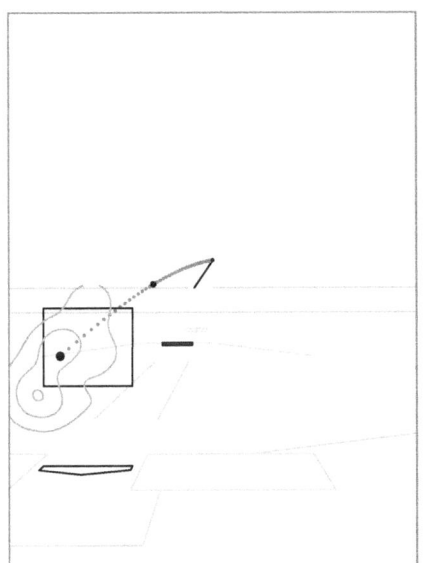

Pitch Shape vs RHH

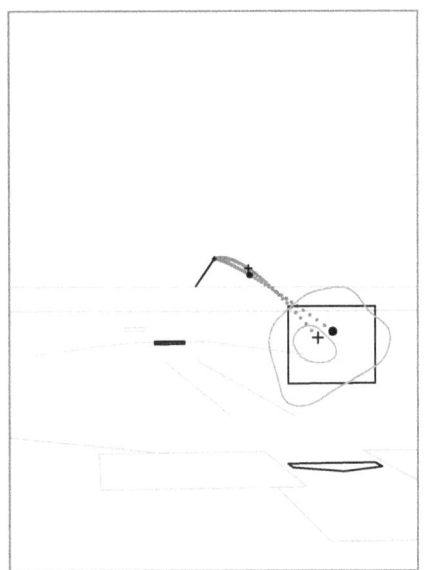

Type		Frequency	Velocity	H Movement	V Movement
●	Fastball	52.5%	91.8 [97]	9.2 [88]	-14.4 [102]
+	Cutter	18.0%	87.3 [93]	-1.2 [95]	-24.8 [98]
▲	Changeup	4.5%	84.4 [97]	12.8 [94]	-27.4 [100]
▽	Slider	16.8%	84.1 [101]	-2.8 [91]	-32.2 [104]
◇	Curveball	8.2%	75.3 [87]	-3.8 [85]	-50.2 [96]

Josh Lindblom RHP

Born: 06/15/87   Age: 34   Bats: R   Throws: R
Height: 6'4"   Weight: 240   Origin: Round 2, 2008 Draft (#61 overall)

YEAR	TEAM	LVL	AGE	W	L	SV	G	GS	IP	H	HR	BB/9	K/9	K	GB%	BABIP
2020	MIL	MLB	33	2	4	0	12	10	45^1	42	6	3.2	10.3	52	27.5%	.316
2021 FS	MIL	MLB	34	9	8	0	26	26	150	141	28	2.8	8.9	147	31.7%	.283
2021 DC	MIL	MLB	34	8	8	0	27	27	137.7	130	26	2.8	8.9	135	31.7%	.283

Comparables: Anthony Swarzak, Jared Hughes, Andrew Miller

There's danger in reading too much into any performance in 2020, because of everything from the length of the season to the circumstances under which it was played. Lindblom struggled in his reentry into Stateside baseball, but all of the reasons why he was attractive remained in evidence. His high-spin four-seamer opens up the top of the zone, though his mechanics make it a bit tough for him to consistently spot it there. He has a good cutter and two variants on his changeup, including a splitter that was instrumental to his KBO revival. His slider is a bit slurvy, but it works. He just needs better luck.

YEAR	TEAM	LVL	AGE	WHIP	ERA	DRA-	WARP	MPH	FB%	WHF	CSP
2020	MIL	MLB	33	1.28	5.16	111	0.1	91.5	35.1%	29.8%	
2021 FS	MIL	MLB	34	1.26	4.24	97	1.7	91.5	35.1%	29.8%	42.9%
2021 DC	MIL	MLB	34	1.26	4.24	97	1.5	91.5	35.1%	29.8%	42.9%

Josh Lindblom, continued

Pitch Shape vs LHH

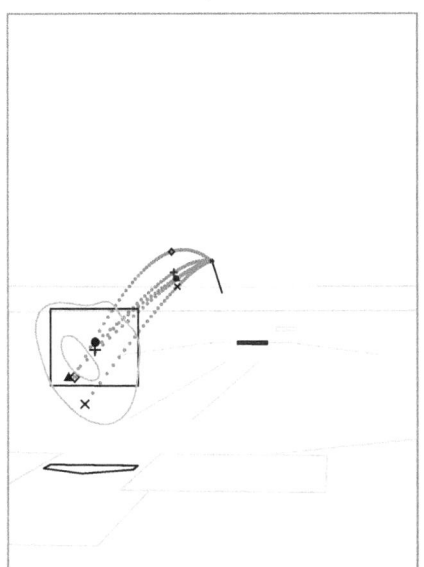

Pitch Shape vs RHH

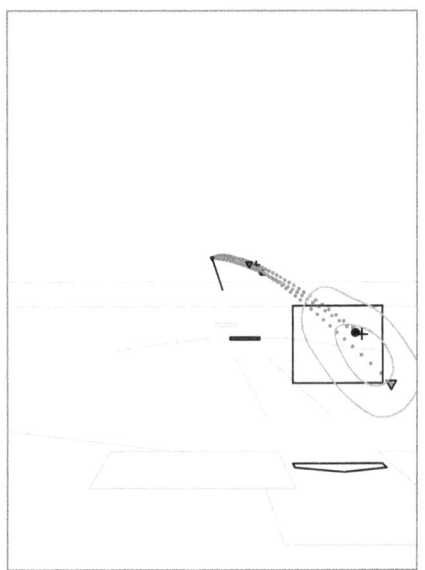

Type	Frequency	Velocity	H Movement	V Movement
● Fastball	34.8%	90.3 [93]	-4.5 [111]	-14.9 [101]
+ Cutter	19.1%	85.9 [85]	3.1 [108]	-24.9 [97]
▲ Changeup	9.1%	84.3 [97]	-13.1 [93]	-26.3 [103]
✕ Splitter	10.3%	83.6 [92]	-6.5 [105]	-27.9 [105]
▽ Slider	17.0%	76.1 [65]	14.4 [134]	-42.6 [74]
◇ Curveball	9.5%	71.3 [71]	14.4 [128]	-60.7 [72]

Hoby Milner LHP

Born: 01/13/91 Age: 30 Bats: L Throws: L
Height: 6'3" Weight: 175 Origin: Round 7, 2012 Draft (#248 overall)

YEAR	TEAM	LVL	AGE	W	L	SV	G	GS	IP	H	HR	BB/9	K/9	K	GB%	BABIP
2018	DUR	AAA	27	1	0	2	15	1	14^1	14	1	1.9	13.2	21	40.0%	.394
2018	LHV	AAA	27	0	0	0	25	0	26^1	21	2	4.8	9.6	28	44.1%	.288
2018	PHI	MLB	27	0	0	0	10	0	4^2	6	1	5.8	7.7	4	41.2%	.312
2018	TB	MLB	27	0	0	0	4	0	2^2	3	2	6.8	13.5	4	14.3%	.200
2019	DUR	AAA	28	3	3	12	50	0	61^2	47	7	1.9	13.0	89	43.2%	.305
2019	TB	MLB	28	0	0	0	4	0	3^2	4	0	2.5	7.4	3	25.0%	.333
2020	LAA	MLB	29	0	0	0	19	0	13^1	13	5	4.0	8.8	13	38.5%	.235
2021 FS	MIL	MLB	30	2	2	0	57	0	50	43	6	2.9	9.8	54	39.5%	.287

Comparables: Nick Wittgren, Tyler Webb, Ryan Weber

A nominal LOOGy, you'd hope Milner was better against sinistral batters than a .678 career OPS allowed. Sure, that's .067 points better than the league average since Milner's 2017 debut, but also smaller than the margin between league average and Milner's OPS against all batters. Much like his initials, it's enough to make you go hm.

YEAR	TEAM	LVL	AGE	WHIP	ERA	DRA-	WARP	MPH	FB%	WHF	CSP
2018	DUR	AAA	27	1.19	3.77	73	0.2				
2018	LHV	AAA	27	1.33	2.39	84	0.3				
2018	PHI	MLB	27	1.93	7.71	187	-0.2	91.3	69.8%	10.8%	
2018	TB	MLB	27	1.88	6.75	214	-0.1	90.4	62.5%	26.9%	
2019	DUR	AAA	28	0.97	3.06	38	2.6				
2019	TB	MLB	28	1.36	7.36	109	0.0	89.1	68.6%	14.3%	
2020	LAA	MLB	29	1.43	8.10	106	0.1	89.2	53.8%	19.8%	
2021 FS	MIL	MLB	30	1.20	3.56	84	0.7	89.4	57.7%	18.7%	49.5%

Hoby Milner, continued

Pitch Shape vs LHH

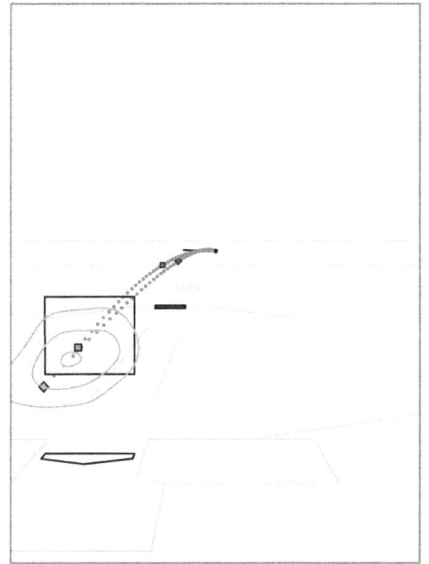

Pitch Shape vs RHH

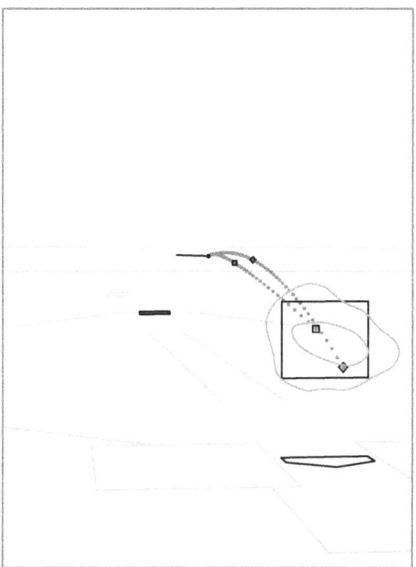

Type	Frequency	Velocity	H Movement	V Movement
☐ Sinker	53.8%	87.9 [77]	13.6 [96]	-26.1 [82]
◇ Curveball	44.1%	77.8 [97]	-13.9 [126]	-41.1 [116]

Milwaukee Brewers 2021

Freddy Peralta RHP

Born: 06/04/96   Age: 25   Bats: R   Throws: R
Height: 5'11"   Weight: 199   Origin: International Free Agent, 2013

YEAR	TEAM	LVL	AGE	W	L	SV	G	GS	IP	H	HR	BB/9	K/9	K	GB%	BABIP
2018	RMV	AAA	22	6	2	0	13	13	61	49	1	4.1	12.8	87	44.7%	.350
2018	MIL	MLB	22	6	4	0	16	14	78¹	49	8	4.6	11.0	96	30.4%	.238
2019	SA	AAA	23	0	0	0	4	0	7	4	0	3.9	21.9	17	25.0%	.500
2019	MIL	MLB	23	7	3	1	39	8	85	87	15	3.9	12.2	115	31.6%	.343
2020	MIL	MLB	24	3	1	0	15	1	29¹	22	2	3.7	14.4	47	33.3%	.333
2021 FS	MIL	MLB	25	10	7	0	26	26	150	115	21	4.0	12.4	206	36.1%	.285
2021 DC	MIL	MLB	25	8	4	0	58	6	80	61	11	4.0	12.4	110	36.1%	.285

Comparables: Phil Hughes, Daniel Norris, Lance McCullers Jr.

Peralta's wild, low-slot crossfire delivery makes his fastball appear not so much a prototypical modern riser as it does an old-fashioned hop ball. The arm action says sinker, but it's never a true sinker, and sometimes it positively jumps up to the hitter's neck or so. That makes him a tough at-bat and enables him to induce plenty of weak contact. He became impossible to handle when he added a slider, a great fit for that delivery, with its cutback and the hip swing to get his back leg over an imaginary picket fence at the end. Peralta is best suited to the bullpen, but he's valuable there as a multi-inning, multi-pitch weapon.

YEAR	TEAM	LVL	AGE	WHIP	ERA	DRA-	WARP	MPH	FB%	WHF	CSP
2018	RMV	AAA	22	1.26	3.10	62	1.8				
2018	MIL	MLB	22	1.14	4.25	116	0.1	93.9	77.6%	26.9%	
2019	SA	AAA	23	1.00	1.29	11	0.4				
2019	MIL	MLB	23	1.46	5.29	101	0.6	97.1	78.4%	29.5%	
2020	MIL	MLB	24	1.16	3.99	67	0.8	95.4	65.8%	39.8%	
2021 FS	MIL	MLB	25	1.22	3.45	79	3.2	95.9	74.9%	31.6%	47.2%
2021 DC	MIL	MLB	25	1.22	3.45	79	1.5	95.9	74.9%	31.6%	47.2%

Freddy Peralta, continued

Pitch Shape vs LHH

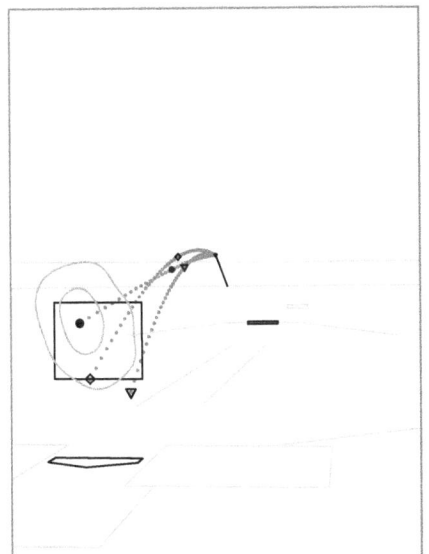

Pitch Shape vs RHH

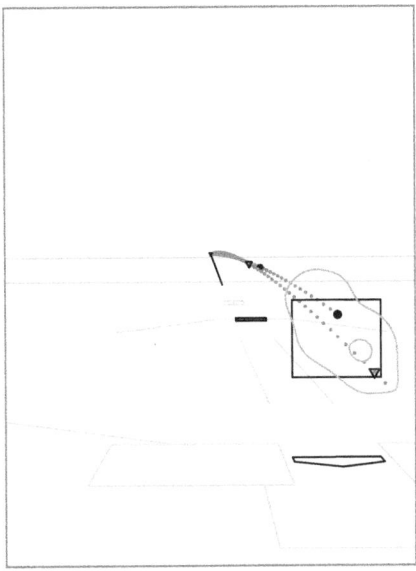

Type	Frequency	Velocity	H Movement	V Movement
● Fastball	65.8%	93.2 [102]	-5.1 [108]	-13.6 [104]
▽ Slider	23.5%	79.8 [82]	13.3 [130]	-39.2 [84]
◇ Curveball	10.7%	75.9 [89]	8.1 [102]	-49.9 [97]

Milwaukee Brewers 2021

Drew Rasmussen   RHP
Born: 07/27/95   Age: 25   Bats: R   Throws: R
Height: 6'1"   Weight: 211   Origin: Round 6, 2018 Draft (#185 overall)

YEAR	TEAM	LVL	AGE	W	L	SV	G	GS	IP	H	HR	BB/9	K/9	K	GB%	BABIP
2019	WIS	LO-A	23	0	0	0	1	1	2	1	0	0.0	13.5	3	66.7%	.333
2019	CAR	HI-A	23	0	0	0	4	4	11^1	7	0	1.6	12.7	16	40.0%	.304
2019	BLX	AA	23	1	3	0	22	18	61	49	4	4.3	11.4	77	46.9%	.321
2020	MIL	MLB	24	1	0	0	12	0	15^1	17	3	5.3	12.3	21	53.7%	.368
2021 FS	MIL	MLB	25	2	2	0	57	0	50	43	6	4.2	10.2	56	45.8%	.292
2021 DC	MIL	MLB	25	2	2	0	53	0	57	49	7	4.2	10.2	65	45.8%	.292

Comparables: Alex Reyes, Cliff Bartosh, Carter Capps

Having already needed two Tommy John surgeries, Rasmussen is wildly unlikely to suddenly turn over a new leaf as a starting pitcher. Oh no, he's a power reliever, all the way, baby. That's why it was odd to see him use two fairly distinct breaking balls and bust out a changeup during his rookie campaign. If that works, great; but in a more realistic scenario, he could take the fastball (which touches triple digits), the slider and an occasionally choked-off change against lefties and blossom into a solid setup man. Not getting lost in the weeds with the twin breaking pitches seems vital.

YEAR	TEAM	LVL	AGE	WHIP	ERA	DRA-	WARP	MPH	FB%	WHF	CSP
2019	WIS	LO-A	23	0.50	0.00	49	0.1				
2019	CAR	HI-A	23	0.79	1.59	52	0.3				
2019	BLX	AA	23	1.28	3.54	88	0.5				
2020	MIL	MLB	24	1.70	5.87	81	0.3	99.2	68.2%	32.0%	
2021 FS	MIL	MLB	25	1.33	3.83	88	0.6	99.2	68.2%	32.0%	45.1%
2021 DC	MIL	MLB	25	1.33	3.83	88	0.7	99.2	68.2%	32.0%	45.1%

Drew Rasmussen, continued

Pitch Shape vs LHH

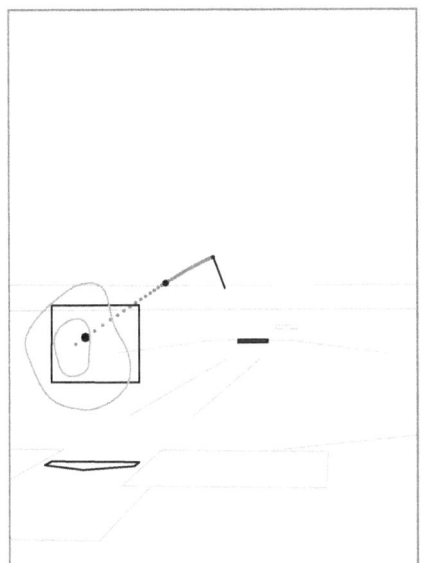

Pitch Shape vs RHH

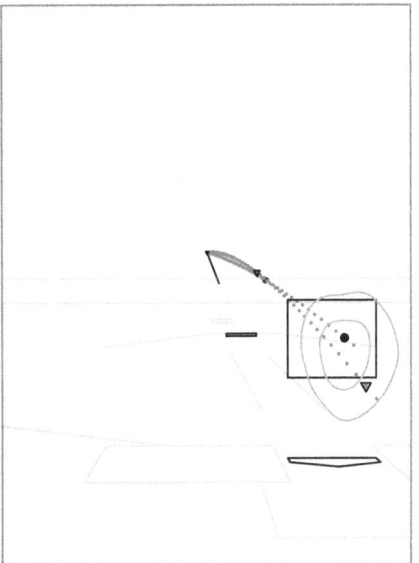

Type	Frequency	Velocity	H Movement	V Movement
● Fastball	68.2%	97.9 [117]	-5.7 [105]	-9.7 [116]
▲ Changeup	4.0%	90 [119]	-10.5 [107]	-18.4 [125]
▽ Slider	17.9%	86.9 [113]	3 [92]	-36.4 [92]
◇ Curveball	9.9%	81.9 [113]	4.6 [88]	-47.3 [103]

Milwaukee Brewers 2021

Brent Suter LHP
Born: 08/29/89 Age: 31 Bats: L Throws: L
Height: 6'4" Weight: 213 Origin: Round 31, 2012 Draft (#965 overall)

YEAR	TEAM	LVL	AGE	W	L	SV	G	GS	IP	H	HR	BB/9	K/9	K	GB%	BABIP
2018	MIL	MLB	28	8	7	0	20	18	101^1	102	18	1.7	7.5	84	32.2%	.286
2019	SA	AAA	29	0	0	0	4	2	11^2	4	0	1.5	13.9	18	40.9%	.190
2019	MIL	MLB	29	4	0	0	9	0	18^1	10	1	0.5	7.4	15	51.0%	.188
2020	MIL	MLB	30	2	0	0	16	4	31^2	30	4	1.4	10.8	38	52.9%	.321
2021 FS	MIL	MLB	31	10	6	0	26	26	150	131	17	1.8	9.3	154	45.0%	.286
2021 DC	MIL	MLB	31	8	4	0	49	9	89.7	78	10	1.8	9.3	92	45.0%	.286

Comparables: Sam Gaviglio, Jacob Barnes, Matt Andriese

Literally leaning into his natural funk, Suter developed a new semi-windup in 2020. He started from a side-saddle set position, then performed a deep drop step, with his right heel getting a couple of feet off toward third base as he bent forward at the waist, his face and glove pointing toward first base. Then came the change of direction, with that right leg swinging up into a high kick, then leading him well toward first base in a crossfire delivery. It's never easy to bully hitters with a fastball that sits in the mid-80s, but Suter managed it, not only with his distracting gesticulations but by tailoring his heat to each batter and each sequence he deployed. Fellow lefties got more sinkers than in the past. Righties got a version of his four-seamer from that wild, angled delivery that might be better classified as a cutter. His changeup firmed up and worked off the heat better. Suter is as smart as he is quirky, and his excellent control forces batters to find a way to barrel something if they want to reach base. Lately, they're not having much luck.

YEAR	TEAM	LVL	AGE	WHIP	ERA	DRA-	WARP	MPH	FB%	WHF	CSP
2018	MIL	MLB	28	1.19	4.44	112	0.3	88.6	68.9%	23.2%	
2019	SA	AAA	29	0.51	0.00	10	0.7				
2019	MIL	MLB	29	0.60	0.49	84	0.2	89.3	78.1%	26.8%	
2020	MIL	MLB	30	1.11	3.13	73	0.7	87.9	79.1%	31.1%	
2021 FS	MIL	MLB	31	1.07	2.77	69	4.0	88.4	74.4%	27.0%	49.0%
2021 DC	MIL	MLB	31	1.07	2.77	69	2.2	88.4	74.4%	27.0%	49.0%

Brent Suter, continued

Pitch Shape vs LHH

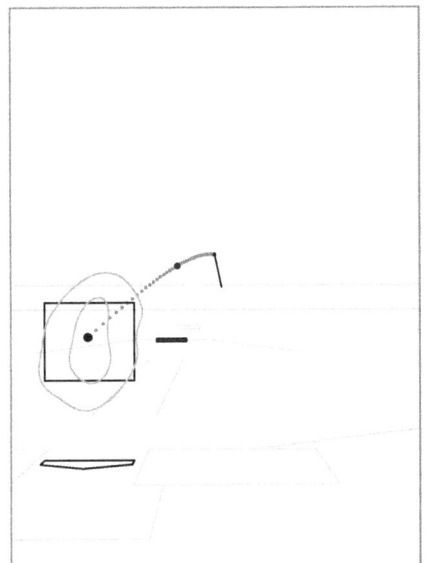

Pitch Shape vs RHH

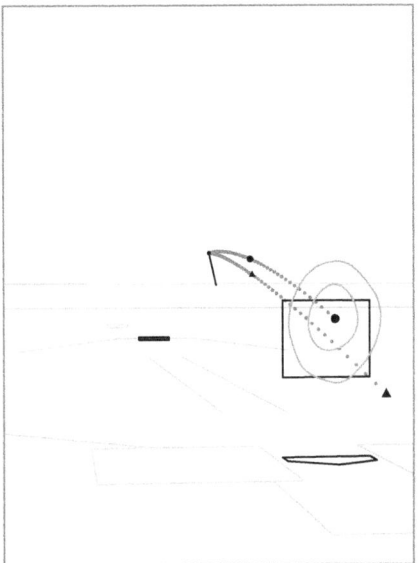

Type	Frequency	Velocity	H Movement	V Movement
● Fastball	71.3%	85.6 [78]	-3.5 [149]	-22.3 [80]
□ Sinker	7.8%	87.4 [74]	8.9 [130]	-21 [99]
▲ Changeup	13.8%	81.4 [85]	10.1 [109]	-27.3 [100]
▽ Slider	7.2%	73.4 [53]	-9.6 [116]	-51.8 [47]

Brewers Player Analysis - 65

Justin Topa RHP

Born: 03/07/91 Age: 30 Bats: R Throws: R
Height: 6'4" Weight: 200 Origin: Round 17, 2013 Draft (#509 overall)

YEAR	TEAM	LVL	AGE	W	L	SV	G	GS	IP	H	HR	BB/9	K/9	K	GB%	BABIP
2018	FRI	AA	27	2	3	0	9	6	41	53	4	2.9	7.5	34	48.1%	.383
2019	CAR	HI-A	28	0	3	3	15	0	16	14	1	1.1	10.7	19	43.2%	.310
2019	BLX	AA	28	0	3	0	18	0	24	22	0	3.0	8.2	22	47.2%	.314
2020	MIL	MLB	29	0	1	0	6	0	7^2	7	1	0.0	14.1	12	55.6%	.353
2021 FS	MIL	MLB	30	2	2	0	57	0	50	46	7	2.9	8.7	48	45.9%	.284
2021 DC	MIL	MLB	30	2	2	0	49	0	50.7	46	7	2.9	8.7	49	45.9%	.284

Comparables: Robert Stock, Matt Dermody, Ryan Mattheus

Stories as winding as Topa's don't usually end in the big leagues. He was undrafted out of high school; a 17th-rounder even as a senior out of Long Island University in 2013; released by the Pirates, then left unprotected by the Rangers and deemed a minor-league free agent after 2018. He didn't even land with a club until Opening Day of 2019. when the Brewers scooped him up. Since then, he's pitched 48 solid innings for them, including eight in the majors in 2020. He strides wide open, throws from a low three-quarters slot and generates excellent separation with a power sinker at 98 mph and a slider that sweeps all the way across the plate. He's a true, late-innings relief weapon, even if it's taken three organizations and seven years to get there.

YEAR	TEAM	LVL	AGE	WHIP	ERA	DRA-	WARP	MPH	FB%	WHF	CSP
2018	FRI	AA	27	1.61	5.71	118	-0.3				
2019	CAR	HI-A	28	1.00	4.50	70	0.2				
2019	BLX	AA	28	1.25	2.62	97	0.0				
2020	MIL	MLB	29	0.91	2.35	72	0.2	99.5	70.3%	26.6%	
2021 FS	MIL	MLB	30	1.24	3.82	90	0.5	99.5	70.3%	26.6%	53.6%
2021 DC	MIL	MLB	30	1.24	3.82	90	0.5	99.5	70.3%	26.6%	53.6%

Justin Topa, continued

Pitch Shape vs LHH

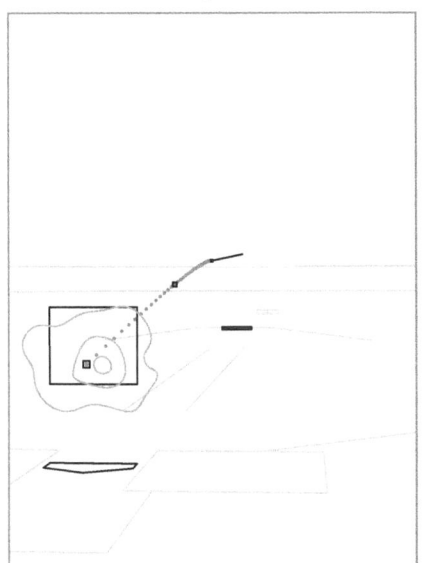

Pitch Shape vs RHH

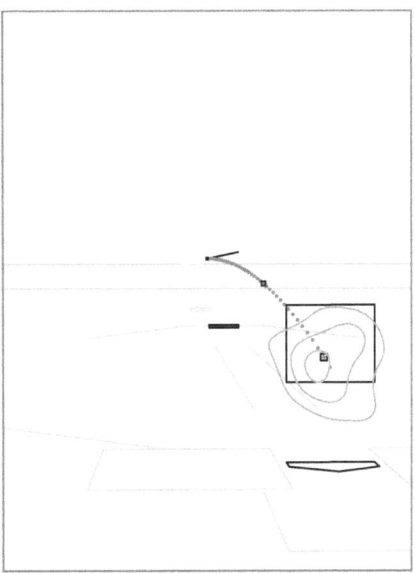

Type	Frequency	Velocity	H Movement	V Movement
☐ Sinker	69.7%	97.8 [128]	-16 [78]	-22.4 [94]
▽ Slider	29.4%	83.5 [98]	14 [133]	-33.6 [100]

Milwaukee Brewers 2021

Devin Williams RHP

Born: 09/21/94   Age: 26   Bats: R   Throws: R
Height: 6'2"   Weight: 200   Origin: Round 2, 2013 Draft (#54 overall)

YEAR	TEAM	LVL	AGE	W	L	SV	G	GS	IP	H	HR	BB/9	K/9	K	GB%	BABIP
2018	CAR	HI-A	23	0	3	0	14	14	34	40	2	5.8	9.3	35	37.3%	.384
2019	BLX	AA	24	7	2	4	31	0	53¹	34	3	4.9	12.8	76	47.4%	.282
2019	MIL	MLB	24	0	0	0	13	0	13²	18	2	4.0	9.2	14	40.0%	.381
2020	MIL	MLB	25	4	1	0	22	0	27	8	1	3.0	17.7	53	61.1%	.200
2021 FS	MIL	MLB	26	2	2	8	57	0	50	38	5	4.2	12.6	70	47.2%	.298
2021 DC	MIL	MLB	26	2	2	8	55	0	57	44	6	4.2	12.6	80	47.2%	.298

Comparables: Elieser Hernandez, Domingo Germán, Yacksel Ríos

There are some ... dare we say "rules" about changeups. They often steer four and a half inches more to the arm side than a pitcher's fastball; they very rarely have a foot of vertical movement relative to the fastball; they almost never have that much movement in both dimensions; and they never, ever do so with a 12-MPH velocity differential. Oh, and they seldom have higher spin rates than the pitcher's heat, and they certainly aren't supposed to have 500 more RPM. Williams' thingamajig defies all the rules. Call it the Airbender. Call it unhittable. Call it a 53-percent strikeout rate wrapped up in a single pitch, the best weapon anyone in the majors has in their arsenal. Just don't call Williams's screwball a changeup.

YEAR	TEAM	LVL	AGE	WHIP	ERA	DRA-	WARP	MPH	FB%	WHF	CSP
2018	CAR	HI-A	23	1.82	5.82	97	0.3				
2019	BLX	AA	24	1.18	2.36	79	0.5				
2019	MIL	MLB	24	1.76	3.95	105	0.0	98.2	61.0%	25.0%	
2020	MIL	MLB	25	0.63	0.33	42	1.1	98.3	43.9%	51.8%	
2021 FS	MIL	MLB	26	1.23	3.24	76	0.9	98.2	48.7%	44.3%	42.5%
2021 DC	MIL	MLB	26	1.23	3.24	76	1.1	98.2	48.7%	44.3%	42.5%

Devin Williams, continued

Pitch Shape vs LHH

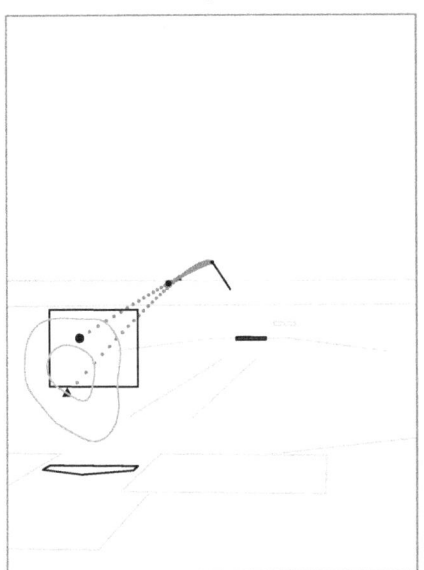

Pitch Shape vs RHH

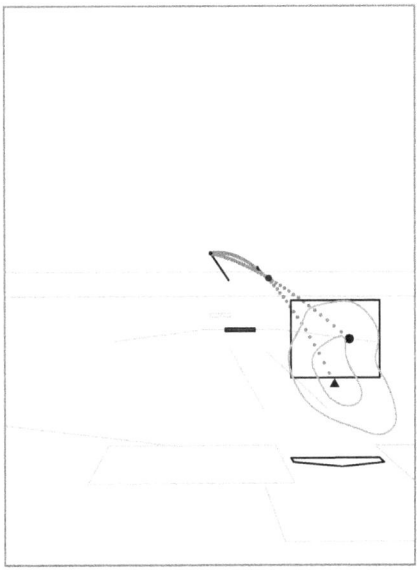

Type	Frequency	Velocity	H Movement	V Movement
● Fastball	43.9%	96.7 [113]	-9.3 [87]	-11.4 [111]
▲ Changeup	52.7%	84.3 [97]	-16.2 [76]	-36.5 [75]
▽ Slider	3.5%	86.7 [112]	5 [99]	-30.8 [108]

Brandon Woodruff RHP

Born: 02/10/93 Age: 28 Bats: L Throws: R
Height: 6'4" Weight: 243 Origin: Round 11, 2014 Draft (#326 overall)

YEAR	TEAM	LVL	AGE	W	L	SV	G	GS	IP	H	HR	BB/9	K/9	K	GB%	BABIP
2018	RMV	AAA	25	3	2	0	17	17	71^1	67	8	4.0	8.6	68	49.3%	.296
2018	MIL	MLB	25	3	0	1	19	4	42^1	36	4	3.0	10.0	47	54.0%	.294
2019	MIL	MLB	26	11	3	0	22	22	121^2	109	12	2.2	10.6	143	45.1%	.322
2020	MIL	MLB	27	3	5	0	13	13	73^2	55	9	2.2	11.1	91	50.0%	.269
2021 FS	MIL	MLB	28	10	6	0	26	26	150	123	15	2.9	10.7	177	47.7%	.291
2021 DC	MIL	MLB	28	10	7	0	27	27	151.3	124	15	2.9	10.7	179	47.7%	.291

Comparables: Daniel Mengden, Joe Musgrove, Zach Davies

We no longer have to wonder what role Woodruff will fill. He's a starter, and he slots comfortably into the upper half of even a very good rotation. His control has never been bad, but his command has come a long way recently. That said, he achieved his modest gains in 2020 by becoming a two-fastball pitcher and leaning more heavily on the changeup. It's not hard to see how he's locating more efficiently, given that he's throwing his breaking stuff less often. The tweak he made to his four-seamer to create separation from the sinker made that pitch a bit easier to square up, and the sinker itself misses bats only the way most sinkers do (which is to say infrequently). In 2021, he'll have to find the feel to get back to trusting his breaking balls so he can evade lumber when it proves necessary.

YEAR	TEAM	LVL	AGE	WHIP	ERA	DRA-	WARP	MPH	FB%	WHF	CSP
2018	RMV	AAA	25	1.39	4.04	95	0.9				
2018	MIL	MLB	25	1.18	3.61	70	0.9	97.5	64.1%	25.3%	
2019	MIL	MLB	26	1.14	3.62	66	3.4	98.1	64.1%	25.5%	
2020	MIL	MLB	27	0.99	3.05	70	1.9	98.3	65.1%	29.0%	
2021 FS	MIL	MLB	28	1.15	2.92	70	4.0	98.1	64.5%	27.0%	49.7%
2021 DC	MIL	MLB	28	1.15	2.92	70	3.9	98.1	64.5%	27.0%	49.7%

Brandon Woodruff, continued

Pitch Shape vs LHH

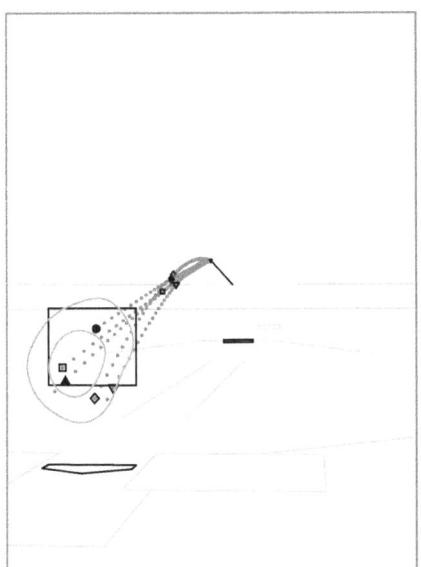

Pitch Shape vs RHH

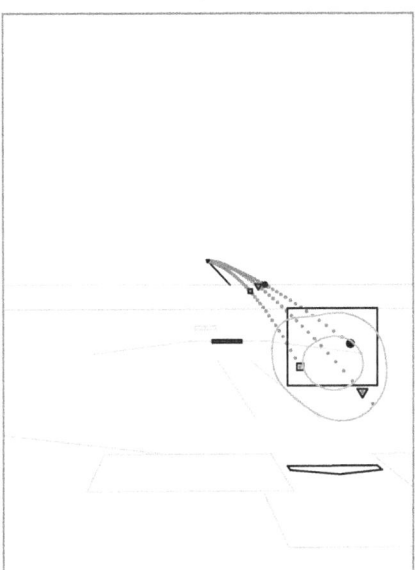

Type	Frequency	Velocity	H Movement	V Movement
● Fastball	34.5%	96.8 [114]	-5.9 [104]	-10.8 [112]
□ Sinker	30.6%	96.5 [121]	-12.4 [105]	-14.5 [120]
▲ Changeup	17.6%	87 [107]	-13.8 [89]	-24.1 [109]
▽ Slider	10.8%	88.4 [120]	2.5 [90]	-30.4 [110]
◇ Curveball	6.5%	83.8 [120]	3.4 [83]	-43.8 [110]

Eric Yardley RHP

Born: 08/18/90   Age: 30   Bats: R   Throws: R
Height: 6'0"   Weight: 170   Origin: Undrafted Free Agent, 2013

YEAR	TEAM	LVL	AGE	W	L	SV	G	GS	IP	H	HR	BB/9	K/9	K	GB%	BABIP
2018	SA	AA	27	2	4	0	34	0	39^1	40	2	2.7	6.2	27	62.8%	.325
2018	ELP	AAA	27	3	0	1	14	0	21^2	25	2	2.9	4.2	10	58.4%	.311
2019	ELP	AAA	28	0	2	7	43	0	63^2	60	3	2.0	7.4	52	62.3%	.303
2019	SD	MLB	28	0	1	0	10	0	11^2	12	1	2.3	5.4	7	61.0%	.289
2020	MIL	MLB	29	2	0	0	24	0	23^1	19	2	3.9	7.3	19	62.7%	.262
2021 FS	MIL	MLB	30	2	2	0	57	0	50	49	5	2.9	7.1	39	60.0%	.292
2021 DC	MIL	MLB	30	2	2	0	55	0	57	57	6	2.9	7.1	44	60.0%	.292

Comparables: Mike Morin, Tyler Rogers, Emilio Pagán

Yardley does everything a hurler can do to create deception and force hitters into defensive postures. Namely, he hides the ball for a long time as he begins his delivery and then lets the arm out in a long arc before sweeping it around to his thigh-high, below-sidearm release. Hitters can sometimes hit his sinker hard, and they can sometimes get his slider up in the air; doing both at once, meaning a hard-hit ball in the air, is almost out of the question. If he had any command of the slider, he'd be truly devastating, but it might cost him too much of that funk to get there. As it stands, he's a solid middle reliever and a future standout on one of those nightmare-fuel Arm Clock graphics.

YEAR	TEAM	LVL	AGE	WHIP	ERA	DRA-	WARP	MPH	FB%	WHF	CSP
2018	SA	AA	27	1.32	3.43	83	0.4				
2018	ELP	AAA	27	1.48	5.40	91	0.2				
2019	ELP	AAA	28	1.16	2.83	41	2.6				
2019	SD	MLB	28	1.29	2.31	89	0.1	87.6	67.4%	22.7%	
2020	MIL	MLB	29	1.24	1.54	89	0.3	89.5	65.1%	19.0%	
2021 FS	MIL	MLB	30	1.31	3.98	93	0.4	89.0	65.6%	19.9%	46.3%
2021 DC	MIL	MLB	30	1.31	3.98	93	0.5	89.0	65.6%	19.9%	46.3%

Eric Yardley, continued

Pitch Shape vs LHH

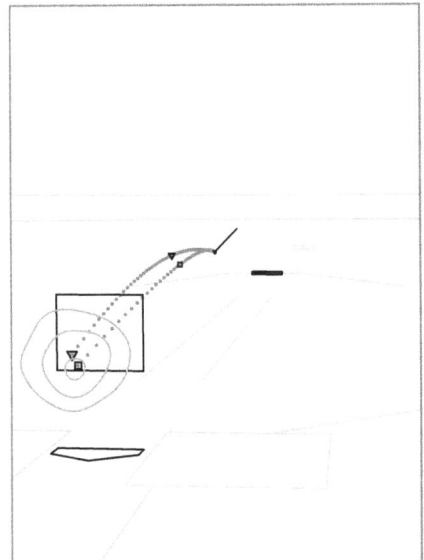

Pitch Shape vs RHH

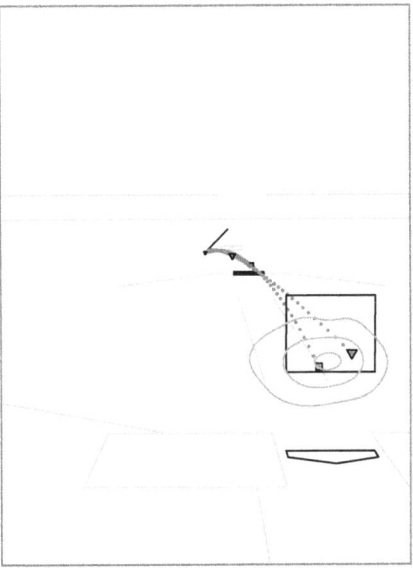

Type	Frequency	Velocity	H Movement	V Movement
☐ Sinker	64.0%	88 [77]	-15.1 [85]	-37.8 [44]
▽ Slider	33.6%	73.2 [52]	14.2 [134]	-36.4 [92]

Milwaukee Brewers 2021

PLAYER COMMENTS WITHOUT GRAPHS

Tyler Austin 1B
Born: 09/06/91 Age: 29 Bats: R Throws: R
Height: 6'2" Weight: 220 Origin: Round 13, 2010 Draft (#415 overall)

YEAR	TEAM	LVL	AGE	PA	R	2B	3B	HR	RBI	BB	K	SB	CS	AVG/OBP/SLG
2018	ROC	AAA	26	40	6	2	1	3	8	1	10	0	0	.263/.300/.605
2018	SWB	AAA	26	108	14	9	0	6	14	8	32	0	0	.253/.315/.525
2018	NYY	MLB	26	132	16	6	0	8	23	8	53	1	1	.223/.280/.471
2018	MIN	MLB	26	136	18	4	0	9	24	11	42	0	1	.236/.294/.488
2019	SA	AAA	27	63	15	3	0	4	10	8	17	3	1	.333/.413/.611
2019	MIN	MLB	27	5	1	1	0	0	0	1	3	0	0	.250/.400/.500
2019	SF	MLB	27	147	24	2	1	8	20	17	57	1	0	.185/.279/.400
2019	MIL	MLB	27	27	5	2	0	1	4	6	7	1	0	.200/.370/.450
2021 FS	MIL	MLB	29	600	71	21	2	29	81	60	219	2	1	.209/.294/.421

Comparables: Joe Koshansky, Mitch Jones, Christian Walker

In his second bayside franchise and country in as many years, the former Yankees prospect clobbered the second-most dingers on the team, despite missing nearly half the season. He did even better on a rate basis, as he led all NPB hitters with at least 200 plate appearances in ISO and was in the 75th percentile in OBP. However, this likely overperformance of his true talent in an abbreviated campaign means he is doomed to fail to meet the unreasonably high expectations from the fans and media alike. He may want to have a talk with another former Yankee acquainted with the perils of the small sample, Kevin Maas.

YEAR	TEAM	LVL	AGE	PA	DRC+	BABIP	BRR	FRAA	WARP
2018	ROC	AAA	26	40	118	.280	-0.1	1B(7): -0.5	0.0
2018	SWB	AAA	26	108	111	.311	0.0	1B(17): -0.6, RF(2): -0.5, LF(1): 0.1	0.0
2018	NYY	MLB	26	132	95	.311	-0.1	1B(27): -1.3	0.0
2018	MIN	MLB	26	136	100	.270	-0.3	1B(15): 0.1	0.2
2019	SA	AAA	27	63	129	.412	0.1	1B(13): 0.5, LF(1): -0.0	0.3
2019	MIN	MLB	27	5	83	1.000		1B(2): -0.1	0.0
2019	SF	MLB	27	147	81	.246	1.4	LF(22): 2.0, 1B(12): -0.5, RF(3): -0.0	0.3
2019	MIL	MLB	27	27	111	.231	0.4	1B(9): -0.1	0.1
2021 FS	MIL	MLB	29	600	91	.289	-0.4	1B -1, LF 0	0.1

Lorenzo Cain CF

Born: 04/13/86   Age: 35   Bats: R   Throws: R
Height: 6'2"   Weight: 214   Origin: Round 17, 2004 Draft (#496 overall)

YEAR	TEAM	LVL	AGE	PA	R	2B	3B	HR	RBI	BB	K	SB	CS	AVG/OBP/SLG
2018	MIL	MLB	32	620	90	25	2	10	38	71	94	30	7	.308/.395/.417
2019	MIL	MLB	33	623	75	30	0	11	48	50	106	18	8	.260/.325/.372
2020	MIL	MLB	34	21	4	1	0	0	2	3	2	0	0	.333/.429/.389
2021 FS	MIL	MLB	35	600	79	24	1	13	63	52	117	21	6	.260/.333/.385
2021 DC	MIL	MLB	35	568	74	22	1	12	59	49	111	20	6	.260/.333/.385

Comparables: Roberto Kelly, Torii Hunter, Dave Henderson

Cain said that when he opted out of the balance of the season on August 1, it was not only out of fear of COVID-19 but also with a desire to re-establish his faith. It's not a bad idea for the aging center fielder to give a little faith just now; going forward, he'll need to get some from teams. Since 2007, the only center fielders to qualify for the batting title at age 35 or older are Brett Gardner and Mike Cameron. Cain had a season in 2019 that demonstrated why it's so rare for an aging player to stick in center, and now he's set to turn 35 without having had a chance to redeem himself.

YEAR	TEAM	LVL	AGE	PA	DRC+	BABIP	BRR	FRAA	WARP
2018	MIL	MLB	32	620	121	.357	4.3	CF(138): 2.1	4.5
2019	MIL	MLB	33	623	87	.301	1.0	CF(143): -1.6	1.2
2020	MIL	MLB	34	21	104	.375	0.2	CF(5): 0.2	0.1
2021 FS	MIL	MLB	35	600	101	.309	1.0	CF 3	2.4
2021 DC	MIL	MLB	35	568	101	.309	0.9	CF 3	2.2

Mario Feliciano C

Born: 11/20/98 Age: 22 Bats: R Throws: R
Height: 6'1" Weight: 200 Origin: Round 2, 2016 Draft (#75 overall)

YEAR	TEAM	LVL	AGE	PA	R	2B	3B	HR	RBI	BB	K	SB	CS	AVG/OBP/SLG
2018	CAR	HI-A	19	165	20	7	1	3	12	13	59	2	0	.205/.282/.329
2019	CAR	HI-A	20	482	62	25	4	19	81	29	139	2	1	.273/.324/.477
2021 FS	MIL	MLB	22	600	63	22	2	14	67	35	188	2	1	.210/.264/.336
2021 DC	MIL	MLB	22	34	3	1	0	0	3	2	10	0	0	.210/.264/.336

Comparables: Wilin Rosario, Wilson Ramos, Nick Williams

Without full, competitive games against other teams' affiliates, minor-league catchers didn't get the chance to work on managing the flow of a game, situational pitch-calling or other nuances. On the other hand, they did get extra time with a select set of pitchers, and the opportunity to develop a rapport and familiarity with them that might otherwise take years to establish. Feliciano took advantage of the latter in 2020, drawing rave reviews from several hurlers while showing off his very good, power-centric offensive game. Most young prospects saw their roads to the majors elongated by the lost minor-league season; Feliciano might have shortened his.

YEAR	TEAM	LVL	AGE	PA	DRC+	BABIP	BRR	FRAA	WARP
2018	CAR	HI-A	19	165	53	.318	0.5	C(25): -0.6	-0.5
2019	CAR	HI-A	20	482	118	.351	-5.1	C(61): -0.4	1.7
2021 FS	MIL	MLB	22	600	64	.288	-0.4	C 0	-0.4
2021 DC	MIL	MLB	22	34	64	.288	0.0	C 0	0.0

Derek Fisher RF

Born: 08/21/93 Age: 27 Bats: L Throws: R
Height: 6'3" Weight: 215 Origin: Round 1, 2014 Draft (#37 overall)

YEAR	TEAM	LVL	AGE	PA	R	2B	3B	HR	RBI	BB	K	SB	CS	AVG/OBP/SLG
2018	FRE	AAA	24	281	44	12	1	10	34	39	85	11	1	.251/.363/.435
2018	HOU	MLB	24	86	13	2	2	4	11	5	42	2	0	.165/.209/.392
2019	RR	AAA	25	270	44	9	1	14	36	40	67	8	3	.286/.401/.522
2019	HOU	MLB	25	60	9	2	1	1	5	7	14	4	1	.226/.317/.358
2019	TOR	MLB	25	107	14	2	0	6	12	14	43	1	0	.161/.271/.376
2020	TOR	MLB	26	39	5	2	1	1	7	7	11	0	1	.226/.359/.452
2021 FS	MIL	MLB	27	600	82	23	2	25	74	73	209	10	4	.218/.321/.416
2021 DC	MIL	MLB	27	96	13	3	0	4	11	11	33	1	1	.218/.321/.416

Comparables: Dave Nicholson, Brandon Boggs, Ben Johnson

Few ballplayers have incurred such universal, unequivocal fan wrath as Fisher did on September 15, when his three miscues (two back-to-back!) precipitated a 20-run deluge from the Yankees. It's unclear when or if he'll have the opportunity to repay the debt; on a healthy roster, Fisher is a fourth outfielder at best, and his corner-only, low-contact profile isn't really a good fit for the position. In the days of actual benches, his ability to work walks and occasionally run into one would have made for a decent lottery ticket pinch hitter, but that's likely all he is now, and that roster spot got outsourced to the sidearming reliever Fisher would strike out against.

YEAR	TEAM	LVL	AGE	PA	DRC+	BABIP	BRR	FRAA	WARP
2018	FRE	AAA	24	281	113	.347	2.2	CF(33): -2.7, LF(19): -0.7, RF(4): -0.3	0.7
2018	HOU	MLB	24	86	48	.257	1.6	LF(26): -1.3, CF(9): -0.4, RF(3): 0.2	-0.3
2019	RR	AAA	25	270	122	.347	-0.5	CF(29): 1.5, RF(21): 1.5, LF(4): -0.1	1.7
2019	HOU	MLB	25	60	83	.289	1.0	LF(11): -0.0, RF(5): 0.4	0.1
2019	TOR	MLB	25	107	67	.205	-0.4	LF(27): 0.9, RF(4): -0.3, CF(3): -0.2	-0.1
2020	TOR	MLB	26	39	98	.300	0.1	RF(10): -0.5, LF(5): -0.9	0.0
2021 FS	MIL	MLB	27	600	100	.310	0.4	LF -1, RF 0	1.6
2021 DC	MIL	MLB	27	96	100	.310	0.1	LF 0, RF 0	0.2

Milwaukee Brewers 2021

Eduardo Garcia SS
Born: 07/10/02 Age: 18 Bats: R Throws: R
Height: 6'2" Weight: 160 Origin: International Free Agent, 2019

YEAR	TEAM	LVL	AGE	PA	R	2B	3B	HR	RBI	BB	K	SB	CS	AVG/OBP/SLG
2019	DSL BRW	ROK	16	40	6	2	0	1	3	6	9	1	1	.312/.450/.469
2021								No projection						

Garcia, a lanky and toolsy shortstop, held his own at the Brewers' alternate site—an impressive feat for a player born just after Milwaukee hosted the 2002 All-Star Game.

YEAR	TEAM	LVL	AGE	PA	DRC+	BABIP	BRR	FRAA	WARP
2019	DSL BRW	ROK	16	40		.409			
2021					No projection				

Payton Henry C
Born: 06/24/97 Age: 24 Bats: R Throws: R
Height: 6'2" Weight: 215 Origin: Round 6, 2016 Draft (#171 overall)

YEAR	TEAM	LVL	AGE	PA	R	2B	3B	HR	RBI	BB	K	SB	CS	AVG/OBP/SLG
2018	WIS	LO-A	21	389	44	15	2	10	41	38	124	1	3	.234/.327/.380
2019	CAR	HI-A	22	482	49	22	1	14	75	26	142	1	1	.242/.315/.395
2021 FS	MIL	MLB	24	600	52	22	1	14	57	39	229	0	1	.190/.259/.315

Comparables: Eric Haase, Zach Green, Jose Lobaton

There's something pleasingly blue-collar about Henry's name. It fits a middle-tier catching prospect like a custom-made chest protector. Henry has made a name for himself, too, by making steady progress as both a powerful hitter and a sturdy, strong-armed receiver. Most middle-tier catching prospects end up being pulled off the shelves and dumped into the backup backstop bargain bin, though. Barring a swing and approach change focused on a quicker load and earlier, better swing decisions, Henry's profile (and his name) will both fit well there, too.

YEAR	TEAM	LVL	AGE	PA	DRC+	BABIP	BRR	FRAA	WARP
2018	WIS	LO-A	21	389	100	.335	-2.5	C(93): 1.4	1.1
2019	CAR	HI-A	22	482	98	.324	-2.5	C(67): 2.4	1.4
2021 FS	MIL	MLB	24	600	58	.295	-0.9	C -1	-1.0

Cooper Hummel OF

Born: 11/28/94   Age: 26   Bats: S   Throws: R
Height: 5'10"   Weight: 198   Origin: Round 18, 2016 Draft (#531 overall)

YEAR	TEAM	LVL	AGE	PA	R	2B	3B	HR	RBI	BB	K	SB	CS	AVG/OBP/SLG
2018	CAR	HI-A	23	404	51	25	0	8	50	63	93	3	1	.260/.397/.410
2019	BLX	AA	24	419	62	8	5	17	56	62	100	4	7	.249/.384/.450
2021 FS	MIL	MLB	26	600	64	22	2	17	65	70	178	1	1	.213/.319/.368

Comparables: Fernando Perez, Steven Souza Jr., John Raynor

Looking for a developmental reset button, converted outfielder Cooper Hummel tried to slide back behind the plate in 2020. He might stick there this time, but only because teams will let almost anyone soak up innings at catcher in the minor leagues.

YEAR	TEAM	LVL	AGE	PA	DRC+	BABIP	BRR	FRAA	WARP
2018	CAR	HI-A	23	404	136	.339	-1.5	LF(28): -1.8, RF(23): -0.5, C(8): -0.4	1.0
2019	BLX	AA	24	419	138	.301	-1.1	LF(75): 6.3, RF(4): 0.5	3.2
2021 FS	MIL	MLB	26	600	93	.287	-0.6	LF 7, RF 0	1.7

Tristen Lutz OF

Born: 08/22/98   Age: 22   Bats: R   Throws: R
Height: 6'2"   Weight: 210   Origin: Round 1, 2017 Draft (#34 overall)

YEAR	TEAM	LVL	AGE	PA	R	2B	3B	HR	RBI	BB	K	SB	CS	AVG/OBP/SLG
2018	WIS	LO-A	19	503	63	33	3	13	63	46	139	9	3	.245/.321/.421
2019	CAR	HI-A	20	477	62	24	3	13	54	46	137	3	2	.255/.335/.419
2021 FS	MIL	MLB	22	600	53	23	2	15	60	36	214	2	1	.202/.260/.336

Comparables: Michael Saunders, Yorman Rodriguez, Jordan Schafer

A 2020 minor-league season likely would have seen Lutz reach Double-A, and thus face the superior arms who might fully exploit his strikeout-prone profile. Then again, it might also have seen him finally tap fully into his power, especially after offseason surgery to repair a sports hernia gave way to a strong spring training. Instead, Lutz languished at the alternate site, still swinging and missing too much but showing plenty of athletic ability and potential pop. His big test has been pushed back to 2021.

YEAR	TEAM	LVL	AGE	PA	DRC+	BABIP	BRR	FRAA	WARP
2018	WIS	LO-A	19	503	114	.322	-0.9	RF(68): -11.4, LF(29): 1.9, CF(14): -2.9	-0.2
2019	CAR	HI-A	20	477	108	.343	-1.5	CF(71): -3.0, RF(39): -2.4	0.9
2021 FS	MIL	MLB	22	600	62	.297	-0.3	RF -1, CF 0	-1.7

Milwaukee Brewers 2021

Luke Maile C
Born: 02/06/91 Age: 30 Bats: R Throws: R
Height: 6'3" Weight: 225 Origin: Round 8, 2012 Draft (#272 overall)

YEAR	TEAM	LVL	AGE	PA	R	2B	3B	HR	RBI	BB	K	SB	CS	AVG/OBP/SLG
2018	TOR	MLB	27	231	22	13	1	3	27	25	67	2	0	.248/.333/.366
2019	TOR	MLB	28	129	9	2	1	2	9	8	33	1	0	.151/.205/.235
2021 FS	MIL	MLB	30	600	62	22	2	13	58	46	166	2	1	.204/.273/.327
2021 DC	MIL	MLB	30	30	3	1	0	0	2	2	8	0	0	.204/.273/.327

Comparables: Joel Skinner, Mike DiFelice, Paul Bako

The Brewers are the latest team seeking to score and allow fewer runs by employing Maile as their backup catcher. Has anybody ever seen Maile and Jeff Mathis in the same room? If not, can someone please check on Mathis?

YEAR	TEAM	P. COUNT	FRM RUNS	BLK RUNS	THRW RUNS	TOT RUNS
2018	TOR	9173	8.1	0.1	0.1	8.3
2019	TOR	6007	5.2	0.8	0.3	6.3
2021	MIL	1202	0.9	0.1	0.0	1.1
2021	MIL	1202	0.9	0.1	0.0	1.0

YEAR	TEAM	LVL	AGE	PA	DRC+	BABIP	BRR	FRAA	WARP
2018	TOR	MLB	27	231	84	.351	0.2	C(66): 9.5	1.7
2019	TOR	MLB	28	129	54	.190	-0.2	C(44): 7.2, P(2): -0.0	0.6
2021 FS	MIL	MLB	30	600	66	.267	-0.5	C 18, 1B 0	1.7
2021 DC	MIL	MLB	30	30	66	.267	0.0	C 1	0.1

Garrett Mitchell OF
Born: 09/04/98 Age: 22 Bats: L Throws: R
Height: 6'3" Weight: 215 Origin: Round 1, 2020 Draft (#20 overall)

Milwaukee's extremely value-focused draft strategy paid off when Mitchell, inexplicably, slid all the way to the 20th pick. Though a collegiate position player faces pressure to demonstrate immediate polish and produce quickly, Mitchell has shown that capacity. He lacks power right now but has a swing that could eventually actualize it. He runs more than well enough to play center field for most of the next decade. A good approach and solid contact skills set a high floor for his offensive output. Particularly in the changing world of player development and Minor League Baseball, Mitchell should be a rapid riser.

Hedbert Perez OF
Born: 04/04/03 Age: 18 Bats: L Throws: L
Height: 5'10" Weight: 160 Origin: International Free Agent, 2019

Perez, a teenage toolshed, has big-league bloodlines and a ton of upside, which gave the Brewers both the confidence and the incentive needed to carry a very green prospect at their alternate site last summer.

Jace Peterson 3B
Born: 05/09/90 Age: 31 Bats: L Throws: R
Height: 6'0" Weight: 215 Origin: Round 1, 2011 Draft (#58 overall)

YEAR	TEAM	LVL	AGE	PA	R	2B	3B	HR	RBI	BB	K	SB	CS	AVG/OBP/SLG
2018	NYY	MLB	28	11	0	0	0	0	0	1	3	0	1	.300/.364/.300
2018	BAL	MLB	28	235	21	13	2	3	28	30	55	13	2	.195/.308/.325
2019	NOR	AAA	29	377	58	25	5	10	46	46	56	13	3	.313/.398/.512
2019	BAL	MLB	29	108	14	3	1	2	11	6	24	4	1	.220/.269/.330
2020	MIL	MLB	30	61	6	1	0	2	5	15	20	1	0	.200/.393/.356
2021 FS	MIL	MLB	31	600	61	23	3	13	60	78	152	10	4	.213/.321/.351

Comparables: Damian Jackson, Daniel Descalso, Tony Graffanino

Long-ago first rounder Jace Peterson seems to have stalled out as a utility man playing on minor-league deals, but he did tweak his swing (more torque, better lift to the pull field) and approach (extreme patience) successfully.

YEAR	TEAM	LVL	AGE	PA	DRC+	BABIP	BRR	FRAA	WARP
2018	NYY	MLB	28	11	73	.429	-0.3	LF(2): -0.2, RF(1): -0.0	-0.1
2018	BAL	MLB	28	235	76	.252	1.3	3B(35): 1.9, LF(21): -0.4, 2B(18): -0.5	0.2
2019	NOR	AAA	29	377	130	.350	-0.9	3B(38): 1.2, 1B(26): 1.8, 2B(9): 2.6	2.7
2019	BAL	MLB	29	108	79	.267	0.7	LF(18): 3.3, 3B(9): -0.0, 2B(5): 0.7	0.5
2020	MIL	MLB	30	61	97	.292	-0.3	RF(13): -0.9, 1B(4): -0.0, 3B(4): 0.3	0.0
2021 FS	MIL	MLB	31	600	86	.275	0.5	3B 1, LF 1	0.6

Corey Ray CF
Born: 09/22/94 Age: 26 Bats: L Throws: L
Height: 6'0" Weight: 196 Origin: Round 1, 2016 Draft (#5 overall)

YEAR	TEAM	LVL	AGE	PA	R	2B	3B	HR	RBI	BB	K	SB	CS	AVG/OBP/SLG
2018	BLX	AA	23	600	86	32	7	27	74	60	176	37	7	.239/.323/.477
2019	BLX	AA	24	46	5	3	0	0	0	6	14	3	2	.250/.348/.325
2019	SA	AAA	24	230	23	8	0	7	21	20	89	3	1	.188/.261/.329
2021 FS	MIL	MLB	26	600	61	23	3	14	62	48	225	14	5	.185/.256/.316
2021 DC	MIL	MLB	26	136	14	5	0	3	14	10	51	2	2	.185/.256/.316

Comparables: Melky Mesa, Tommy Pham, Keon Broxton

Milwaukee Brewers 2021

The Brewers were more secretive than most clubs about what happened at their alternate site, electing not to share data or video with other teams for scouting purposes and limiting what they shared via social media. Ray is one of the players who doesn't mind that. Now 26, the former top-five pick still has more first names than solid seasons in the minors, and his major flaws (an overly long swing and deficient pitch recognition) were in evidence even against his team's less-than-elite minor-league arms. He doesn't have another year of too many strikeouts and too few hits hanging on his résumé, but he's still a year closer to officially becoming a bust.

YEAR	TEAM	LVL	AGE	PA	DRC+	BABIP	BRR	FRAA	WARP
2018	BLX	AA	23	600	117	.303	0.5	CF(125): 1.8, LF(6): 1.4, RF(3): 0.5	2.4
2019	BLX	AA	24	46	115	.385	0.1	CF(10): 1.6, LF(1): -0.2	0.4
2019	SA	AAA	24	230	44	.283	-0.4	CF(41): -5.0, RF(8): -1.3, LF(2): -0.3	-1.2
2021 FS	MIL	MLB	26	600	53	.283	1.3	CF 2, RF 0	-1.5
2021 DC	MIL	MLB	26	136	53	.283	0.3	CF 0, RF 0	-0.4

Eric Sogard 2B
Born: 05/22/86 Age: 35 Bats: L Throws: R
Height: 5'10" Weight: 180 Origin: Round 2, 2007 Draft (#81 overall)

YEAR	TEAM	LVL	AGE	PA	R	2B	3B	HR	RBI	BB	K	SB	CS	AVG/OBP/SLG
2018	RMV	AAA	32	101	10	4	0	0	11	10	16	0	1	.225/.297/.270
2018	MIL	MLB	32	113	7	3	0	0	2	12	23	3	0	.134/.241/.165
2019	BUF	AAA	33	38	7	2	0	1	6	7	4	0	0	.267/.395/.433
2019	TOR	MLB	33	323	45	17	2	10	30	29	47	6	0	.300/.362/.477
2019	TB	MLB	33	119	14	6	0	3	10	9	16	2	0	.266/.328/.404
2020	MIL	MLB	34	128	10	5	0	1	10	11	20	0	0	.209/.281/.278
2021 FS	MIL	MLB	35	600	60	26	1	12	60	57	106	7	3	.241/.320/.369

Comparables: Mike Gallego, Jerry Hairston, Bernie Allen

While the temptation to ascribe all of Sogard's power surge in 2019 to the aeroball is understandable, it was probably something closer to being within his control, yet further from being sustainable: good luck. He specializes in lowish but lofted line drives, balls that often fall in front of outfielders when hit softly but can split gaps or clear fences when he happens to really rip into a pitch. A pitcher must make a bad mistake in a bad count for Sogard to find that power. His 2020 line reflects some of the other kind of luck, though, and he's better than those numbers suggest. Alas, he's about to turn 35 and has dealt with nagging lower-leg injuries. There's a fair chance he might never again get to put his skills on full display.

YEAR	TEAM	LVL	AGE	PA	DRC+	BABIP	BRR	FRAA	WARP
2018	RMV	AAA	32	101	62	.267	1.6	2B(18): 1.2, SS(5): 1.2	0.2
2018	MIL	MLB	32	113	72	.173	0.3	SS(24): 0.0, 2B(22): 0.1, LF(1): -0.2	0.1
2019	BUF	AAA	33	38	118	.269	0.7	3B(5): 0.6, 2B(2): 0.4	0.3
2019	TOR	MLB	33	323	112	.326	3.0	2B(43): -1.4, 3B(6): 1.7, RF(6): 0.3	1.7
2019	TB	MLB	33	119	104	.289	-0.1	2B(31): 0.7	0.5
2020	MIL	MLB	34	128	92	.242	-0.1	3B(30): 4.3, 2B(9): 0.1, SS(7): -0.1	0.6
2021 FS	MIL	MLB	35	600	89	.279	-0.2	2B 2, 3B 2	1.2

Brice Turang SS

Born: 11/21/99 Age: 21 Bats: L Throws: R
Height: 6'0" Weight: 173 Origin: Round 1, 2018 Draft (#21 overall)

YEAR	TEAM	LVL	AGE	PA	R	2B	3B	HR	RBI	BB	K	SB	CS	AVG/OBP/SLG
2018	BRG	ROK	18	57	11	2	0	0	7	9	6	8	1	.319/.421/.362
2019	WIS	LO-A	19	357	57	13	4	2	31	49	54	21	4	.287/.384/.376
2019	CAR	HI-A	19	207	25	6	2	1	6	34	47	9	1	.200/.338/.276
2021 FS	MIL	MLB	21	600	51	23	3	7	50	52	161	14	4	.221/.292/.316

Comparables: José Peraza, Asdrúbal Cabrera, Jorge Polanco

It's hard to be projected to become a regular, in this day and age, with power that could play at least a grade below average. That's the needle Turang is trying to thread, but he's unusually well-equipped for the task. He's small by 21st-century standards, but he has some explosiveness in all of his actions. He's likely to stick at shortstop for a while; he runs really well, and it's not showcase speed; he wreaks real havoc with his aggressiveness and savvy on the bases; and he also boasts a solid hit tool, including an advanced approach. Losing a full season of competitive reps might have a disproportionate effect on him, but Turang's feel for the game should help him overcome it.

YEAR	TEAM	LVL	AGE	PA	DRC+	BABIP	BRR	FRAA	WARP
2018	BRG	ROK	18	57		.357			
2019	WIS	LO-A	19	357	141	.339	3.2	SS(43): 0.6, 2B(28): 0.9	3.2
2019	CAR	HI-A	19	207	99	.268	1.6	SS(35): -2.6, 2B(5): -0.8	0.6
2021 FS	MIL	MLB	21	600	69	.301	0.8	SS -1, 2B -1	-0.8

Daniel Vogelbach 1B

Born: 12/17/92   Age: 28   Bats: L   Throws: R
Height: 6'0"   Weight: 270   Origin: Round 2, 2011 Draft (#68 overall)

YEAR	TEAM	LVL	AGE	PA	R	2B	3B	HR	RBI	BB	K	SB	CS	AVG/OBP/SLG
2018	TAC	AAA	25	378	54	16	0	20	60	77	59	0	1	.290/.434/.545
2018	SEA	MLB	25	102	9	2	0	4	13	13	26	0	0	.207/.324/.368
2019	SEA	MLB	26	558	73	17	0	30	76	92	149	0	0	.208/.341/.439
2020	MIL	MLB	27	67	13	2	0	4	12	8	18	0	0	.328/.418/.569
2020	TOR	MLB	27	5	0	0	0	0	0	1	2	0	0	.000/.200/.000
2020	SEA	MLB	27	64	3	1	0	2	4	11	13	0	0	.094/.250/.226
2021 FS	MIL	MLB	28	600	84	21	1	26	84	96	158	0	0	.232/.360/.439
2021 DC	MIL	MLB	28	513	71	18	1	22	72	82	135	0	0	.232/.360/.439

Comparables: Tony Solaita, Carlos Delgado, Mike Napoli

The Internet has tried to adopt Vogelbach as an unapologetic beefy slugger, refusing to do anything but swing for the fences. His charisma and his all-over thickness make him seem a bit happy-go-lucky, but in reality, he's a 28-year-old hunk of waiver bait fighting like mad to become something more. In 2020, he implemented a secondary swing geared to take fastballs away to left field. It didn't generate a ton of hits, but it did bring down his whiff rate considerably. Vogelbach's patience, eagerness to use the whole field and big-time power makes him more promising than he should be at this stage of this career.

YEAR	TEAM	LVL	AGE	PA	DRC+	BABIP	BRR	FRAA	WARP
2018	TAC	AAA	25	378	165	.299	-6.0	1B(53): -2.9	1.8
2018	SEA	MLB	25	102	91	.246	0.6	1B(20): -1.1	0.0
2019	SEA	MLB	26	558	117	.232	-1.7	1B(57): -3.2	1.6
2020	MIL	MLB	27	67	102	.417	0.4	1B(2): 0.5	0.2
2020	TOR	MLB	27	5	102	.000			0.0
2020	SEA	MLB	27	64	104	.079	-0.3		0.1
2021 FS	MIL	MLB	28	600	118	.285	-1.0	1B 0	2.1
2021 DC	MIL	MLB	28	513	118	.285	-0.8	1B 0	1.9

Freddy Zamora SS
Born: 11/01/98 Age: 22 Bats: R Throws: R
Height: 6'1" Weight: 190 Origin: Round 2, 2020 Draft (#53 overall)

The Brewers rarely miss a chance to take a well-rounded position player with a high draft pick. It wasn't too surprising to see them jump on Zamora in the second round. He was available only because he missed the short-lived season due to a suspension and ACL injury. If you want to dream on him as an everyday shortstop, you have to do so by hoping his compact swing translates to healthy contact rates and a quick ascension through pro ball, because he's a bit undertooled in terms of both power and speed. His sure hands, good actions and above-average arm will outweigh those issues for only a few years, after which he's a second baseman or maybe a utility player. Still, that package suits what Milwaukee looks for pretty nicely.

Aaron Ashby LHP
Born: 05/24/98 Age: 23 Bats: R Throws: L
Height: 6'2" Weight: 181 Origin: Round 4, 2018 Draft (#125 overall)

YEAR	TEAM	LVL	AGE	W	L	SV	G	GS	IP	H	HR	BB/9	K/9	K	GB%	BABIP
2018	HEL	ROK	20	1	2	1	6	3	20^1	18	3	3.5	8.4	19	48.3%	.273
2018	WIS	LO-A	20	1	1	0	7	7	37^1	40	1	2.2	11.3	47	50.5%	.398
2019	WIS	LO-A	21	3	4	0	11	10	61	47	4	4.1	11.8	80	48.9%	.319
2019	CAR	HI-A	21	2	6	0	13	13	65	54	1	4.4	7.6	55	47.3%	.286
2021 FS	MIL	MLB	23	2	3	0	57	0	50	47	7	5.3	8.5	47	44.9%	.284

Comparables: Patrick Sandoval, Cristian Javier, Brock Burke

Only halfway through the season did Ashby even get an invite to Milwaukee's alternate site, and he wasn't there to audition for a late-season cameo. Rather, the team brought him back (technically to an affiliate where he'd had success in 2019) to continue working with him on a four-pitch mix that packs real promise. He doesn't have front-of-the-rotation projection, but Ashby throws hard enough and repeats an easy delivery well enough to hope that he'll hone his command, get comfortable using all of his stuff and become an innings-eating southpaw. His slider is the pitch to watch; if or when it turns a corner, so will he.

YEAR	TEAM	LVL	AGE	WHIP	ERA	DRA-	WARP	MPH	FB%	WHF	CSP
2018	HEL	ROK	20	1.28	6.20						
2018	WIS	LO-A	20	1.31	2.17	59	1.1				
2019	WIS	LO-A	21	1.23	3.54	91	0.5				
2019	CAR	HI-A	21	1.32	3.46	98	0.2				
2021 FS	MIL	MLB	23	1.53	5.04	113	-0.1				

Milwaukee Brewers 2021

Alec Bettinger RHP
Born: 07/13/95 Age: 25 Bats: R Throws: R
Height: 6'2" Weight: 210 Origin: Round 10, 2017 Draft (#294 overall)

YEAR	TEAM	LVL	AGE	W	L	SV	G	GS	IP	H	HR	BB/9	K/9	K	GB%	BABIP
2018	WIS	LO-A	22	5	4	0	12	11	62^2	59	6	2.4	7.2	50	34.0%	.291
2018	CAR	HI-A	22	1	6	0	13	12	54^2	70	10	2.8	9.2	56	31.4%	.377
2019	BLX	AA	23	5	7	0	26	26	146^1	121	13	2.2	9.7	157	40.4%	.286
2021 FS	MIL	MLB	25	2	3	0	57	0	50	47	8	3.7	8.1	44	39.2%	.280
2021 DC	MIL	MLB	25	2	2	0	24	3	26.3	25	4	3.7	8.1	23	39.2%	.280

Comparables: Nabil Crismatt, Adam Conley, Cy Sneed

The Brewers probably didn't expect much from Bettinger when they selected him as a University of Virginia senior in the 10th round of the 2017 draft. He's since increased his velocity and proved he can command four pitches, suggesting he should have a big-league future.

YEAR	TEAM	LVL	AGE	WHIP	ERA	DRA-	WARP	MPH	FB%	WHF	CSP
2018	WIS	LO-A	22	1.21	3.73	82	1.0				
2018	CAR	HI-A	22	1.59	6.91	118	-0.1				
2019	BLX	AA	23	1.07	3.44	84	1.5				
2021 FS	MIL	MLB	25	1.37	4.51	105	0.1				
2021 DC	MIL	MLB	25	1.37	4.51	105	0.1				

Dylan File RHP
Born: 06/04/96 Age: 25 Bats: R Throws: R
Height: 6'1" Weight: 205 Origin: Round 21, 2017 Draft (#624 overall)

YEAR	TEAM	LVL	AGE	W	L	SV	G	GS	IP	H	HR	BB/9	K/9	K	GB%	BABIP
2018	WIS	LO-A	22	8	10	0	25	25	136^1	152	15	1.8	7.5	114	39.1%	.336
2019	CAR	HI-A	23	6	4	0	12	12	66^1	71	4	0.9	8.5	63	42.4%	.347
2019	BLX	AA	23	9	2	0	14	14	80^2	74	5	1.7	8.1	73	44.4%	.303
2021 FS	MIL	MLB	25	2	2	0	57	0	50	49	8	2.6	7.2	39	42.7%	.280
2021 DC	MIL	MLB	25	3	2	0	18	6	38.3	38	6	2.6	7.2	30	42.7%	.280

Comparables: Tyler Wilson, Tobi Stoner, Matt Bowman

He'll never rank as an elite prospect, but File is more than an anonymous face in a pitching crowd thanks to great control of a four-pitch mix.

YEAR	TEAM	LVL	AGE	WHIP	ERA	DRA-	WARP	MPH	FB%	WHF	CSP
2018	WIS	LO-A	22	1.32	3.96	89	1.7				
2019	CAR	HI-A	23	1.18	3.80	97	0.2				
2019	BLX	AA	23	1.10	2.79	95	0.3				
2021 FS	MIL	MLB	25	1.28	4.27	101	0.2				
2021 DC	MIL	MLB	25	1.28	4.27	101	0.3				

Antoine Kelly LHP

Born: 12/05/99 Age: 21 Bats: L Throws: L
Height: 6'6" Weight: 205 Origin: Round 2, 2019 Draft (#65 overall)

YEAR	TEAM	LVL	AGE	W	L	SV	G	GS	IP	H	HR	BB/9	K/9	K	GB%	BABIP
2019	BRB	ROK	19	0	0	0	9	9	28²	21	0	1.6	12.9	41	43.5%	.339
2019	WIS	LO-A	19	0	1	0	1	1	3	5	2	12.0	12.0	4	44.4%	.500
2021 FS	MIL	MLB	21	2	3	0	57	0	50	45	8	4.8	9.3	51	40.0%	.284

Comparables: Luis Severino, Edwin Escobar, Adrian Morejon

It's easy to make bets on pitchers like Kelly with a second-round pick. If it doesn't pan out, you never look bad; if it does, you look awfully good. Right now, the Brewers look awfully good. Kelly continued to flash triple-digit heat, and he made plenty of the hoped-for strides in developing his slider and changeup at the club's alternate site in 2020. He's not going to knock on the door of the majors right away, but only because there's still time to dream on him as a flamethrowing three-pitch starter. If he does end up in a relief role, he'll be a terror—and soon.

YEAR	TEAM	LVL	AGE	WHIP	ERA	DRA-	WARP	MPH	FB%	WHF	CSP
2019	BRB	ROK	19	0.91	1.26						
2019	WIS	LO-A	19	3.00	18.00	153	-0.1				
2021 FS	MIL	MLB	21	1.45	4.69	108	0.0				

Max Lazar RHP

Born: 06/03/99 Age: 22 Bats: R Throws: R
Height: 6'3" Weight: 185 Origin: Round 11, 2017 Draft (#324 overall)

YEAR	TEAM	LVL	AGE	W	L	SV	G	GS	IP	H	HR	BB/9	K/9	K	GB%	BABIP
2018	HEL	ROK	19	3	3	0	14	14	68	74	7	2.0	7.3	55	43.2%	.313
2019	BRG	ROK	20	0	1	0	3	3	6	4	0	0.0	15.0	10	27.3%	.364
2019	WIS	LO-A	20	7	3	1	19	10	79	67	5	1.7	12.4	109	37.0%	.337
2021 FS	MIL	MLB	22	2	2	0	57	0	50	45	7	3.0	8.5	47	36.0%	.277

Comparables: Luis Perdomo, Demarcus Evans, Joe Musgrove

Projectable righty Lazar doesn't yet have a plus pitch or even average velocity or spin, but he's shown feel and could take off if the heat ticks up.

YEAR	TEAM	LVL	AGE	WHIP	ERA	DRA-	WARP	MPH	FB%	WHF	CSP
2018	HEL	ROK	19	1.31	4.37						
2019	BRG	ROK	20	0.67	1.50						
2019	WIS	LO-A	20	1.04	2.39	74	1.3				
2021 FS	MIL	MLB	22	1.24	3.84	94	0.4				

Milwaukee Brewers 2021

Angel Perdomo   LHP
Born: 05/07/94   Age: 27   Bats: L   Throws: L
Height: 6'8"   Weight: 265   Origin: International Free Agent, 2011

YEAR	TEAM	LVL	AGE	W	L	SV	G	GS	IP	H	HR	BB/9	K/9	K	GB%	BABIP
2018	DUN	HI-A	24	1	5	1	26	12	79^1	68	5	4.0	11.3	100	44.2%	.328
2019	BLX	AA	25	2	0	0	7	0	15^1	6	0	4.7	12.3	21	42.9%	.222
2019	SA	AAA	25	3	2	1	40	0	54	47	8	6.3	14.3	86	32.2%	.358
2020	MIL	MLB	26	0	0	0	3	0	2^2	3	0	23.6	16.9	5	66.7%	.500
2021 FS	MIL	MLB	27	2	3	0	57	0	50	45	8	6.4	11.0	61	39.2%	.302
2021 DC	MIL	MLB	27	2	2	0	49	0	50.7	46	8	6.4	11.0	62	39.2%	.302

Comparables: Stephen Tarpley, Austen Williams, Justin Shafer

Perdomo, a gigantic lefty, has enormous stuff; either the strike zones he throws to are very small, or he has what you might charitably describe as "strike-throwing problems."

YEAR	TEAM	LVL	AGE	WHIP	ERA	DRA-	WARP	MPH	FB%	WHF	CSP
2018	DUN	HI-A	24	1.30	3.63	69	1.7				
2019	BLX	AA	25	0.91	1.17	53	0.4				
2019	SA	AAA	25	1.57	5.17	85	1.1				
2020	MIL	MLB	26	3.75	20.25	87	0.0	96.3	68.2%	36.4%	
2021 FS	MIL	MLB	27	1.61	5.42	114	-0.1	96.3	68.2%	36.4%	38.7%
2021 DC	MIL	MLB	27	1.61	5.42	114	-0.2	96.3	68.2%	36.4%	38.7%

Ethan Small LHP

Born: 02/14/97 Age: 24 Bats: L Throws: L
Height: 6'4" Weight: 215 Origin: Round 1, 2019 Draft (#28 overall)

YEAR	TEAM	LVL	AGE	W	L	SV	G	GS	IP	H	HR	BB/9	K/9	K	GB%	BABIP
2019	BRG	ROK	22	0	0	0	2	2	3	0	0	0.0	15.0	5	50.0%	.000
2019	WIS	LO-A	22	0	2	0	5	5	18	11	0	2.0	15.5	31	30.3%	.333
2021 FS	MIL	MLB	24	2	2	0	57	0	50	44	7	4.4	10.1	56	36.7%	.288

Comparables: Brendan McKay, Brock Burke, Victor González

If this works, it's going to be really fun to watch Small pitch. He's gambled on himself over and over, from trading in a full ride to a small school to walk on at Mississippi State (ignoring pre-draft offers in the low to mid-six figures) to going back for his senior year there after being a 28th-round pick as a junior, despite having had Tommy John surgery in the interim. The bets all paid, though, as Small put up video-game numbers in 2019, was a first-round pick as a result and now looks like a fast mover through the minors. He lacks top-end velocity, but he varies his delivery, hides the ball and uses his long frame to create great extension from a high arm slot. At the alternate site in 2020, he added and worked to polish a slider, which sounds ambitious for a pitcher with his profile. Betting against him has proven to be unwise.

YEAR	TEAM	LVL	AGE	WHIP	ERA	DRA-	WARP	MPH	FB%	WHF	CSP
2019	BRG	ROK	22	0.00	0.00						
2019	WIS	LO-A	22	0.83	1.00	51	0.6				
2021 FS	MIL	MLB	24	1.37	4.31	102	0.2				

Brewers Prospects

The State of the System:
The Brewers system fired a lot of bullets in trades and graduations to build a roster that made the playoffs three years running. Have they fired them all? Well, let's just say for 2021, the rest of the NL Central might be feeling lucky.

The Top Ten:

1 **Brice Turang** **SS** OFP: 55 ETA: Late 2021 / Early 2022
Born: 11/21/99 Age: 21 Bats: L Throws: R Height: 6'0" Weight: 173
Origin: Round 1, 2018 Draft (#21 overall)

The Report: Turang does everything well, but nothing so well that he's cracked national lists yet. In some ways it's a tough profile. He doesn't project for much power, and while he has a good approach and good contact skills, without putting consistent sting on the baseball, pitchers may challenge him further up the ladder, eroding those low minors walk rates. So the offensive profile may come down to the hit tool, which is solid, maybe even plus. You combine that with solid, but probably not plus shortstop defense, and you have a solid regular. But it all has to break right, and he hasn't seen the upper minors and struggled after a promotion to Advanced-A in 2019. He's a plus runner and good on the basepaths, so if Turang is able to get on base at a .350 or so clip, he'll add some extra value there.

Development Track: Turang was at the Brewers alternate site where reports were ... solidly positive. There's more hard contact and he's driving the ball into the gaps, but those doubles aren't turning into home runs yet, and given his frame, I doubt they ever will to any significant extent. Turang remains a perfectly fine shortstop prospect if still a half-step below the Jeremy Peñas and Gerardo Perdomos you find towards the back of the 101.

Variance: High. There may not be a true carrying tool in the profile, so we have just kicked the can down the road another year waiting to see him continue to produce against pitchers outside of the Midwest League.

J.P. Breen's Fantasy Take: It's never a great sign for an organization, at least in terms of dynasty, when the org's No. 1 prospect isn't a top-101 guy. We're talking Nico Hoerner< with a little less on the hit tool. We're talking Andres Gimenez with a little less speed. Ultimately, we're talking about a dude whose absolute upside is a MI slot ... which, in the parlance of my people, uff da.

Milwaukee Brewers 2021

2 **Garrett Mitchell** OF   OFP: 55   ETA: 2023
Born: 09/04/98   Age: 22   Bats: L   Throws: R   Height: 6'3"   Weight: 215
Origin: Round 1, 2020 Draft (#20 overall)

The Report: Depending on which scout you asked prior to the 2020 draft, Mitchell was either one of the most physically-gifted, tooled-up college players they had ever seen, or someone largely overhyped due to mechanical shortcomings. It really is a test of whether the glass is half full or half empty, with both arguments based on equally-considered evidence. Built like a strong safety with a big chest and broad shoulders, Mitchell runs well even given his size, grading out as a plus-plus runner. It helps defensively as there should be no issues staying in center field chasing down balls in the gap. The debate comes down to the swing and if a guy who has every bit of strength you'd expect from a 30-home run slugger will ever show any semblance of moderate game power. Right now Mitchell makes enough contact and uses his speed to take extra bases, but the difference between that player and one who produces what his physical attributes say he can are entirely different things at present.

Development Track: It's not to say the necessary swing changes can't be made. Mitchell's back elbow never gets to a good position for power, and the front shoulder bars his arm out. Both of these swing elements sap a ton of potential out of the bat. In short: His front-side is weak and back-side collapses. The slap and dash approach may work for him, but it just seems odd coming from someone who looks like a middle-of-the-order masher. From a training standpoint there is little left to accomplish with the body. It is now just a matter of what the Brewers player dev and hitting instruction can do to maximize the swing output.

Variance: High. It's all about the bat. If nothing changes to his game the value is derived solely from his glove and legs, and maybe a hit tool that is average.

Major league ETA: 2023

J.P. Breen's Fantasy Take: Mitchell is the dynasty prospect you want from this org. He'll be a guy who is undervalued in prospect circles because he hasn't been as good—or even been the kind of player—that people want him to be. Even if the bat is disappointing, however, we're looking at a glove-and-speed dude who has fantasy relevance from his speed alone. Remember, even Leonys Martin was worth rostering for a handful of years. And if the Brewers are able to develop him at the dish, we're looking at a potential five-category producer.

3 **Aaron Ashby** LHP   OFP: 55   ETA: Mid to Late 2021
Born: 05/24/98   Age: 23   Bats: R   Throws: L   Height: 6'2"   Weight: 181
Origin: Round 4, 2018 Draft (#125 overall)

The Report: Ashby was one of the later additions to the alternate site, but he didn't waste any time making himself known and went on to impress at instructs, too. The lanky lefty improved the velocity on his already above-average fastball, holding mid-90s late into games and touching 98. Paired with a slow curve with nasty, late breaking action, he boasts a one-two punch of plus pitches to keep batters on their toes. He rounds out his four pitch mix with an equally devastating slider and a developing changeup. He's racked up strikeouts, with the ability to tunnel pitches and elicit swings and misses. Unfortunately, sometimes he's racked up walks too.

Development Track: What good is multiple plus pitches if you can't hit your target? Ashby has the stuff, but command issues still linger. He did a better job at keeping the ball in the strike zone and hitting the glove during instructional league. There's signs he's about to turn a corner, but as he rises through the system he'll have to truly refine his command to find success at higher levels. Ashby feels close to making it to the big club, despite the lack of professional experience under his belt; he's got major league caliber pitches and improved upon his biggest weakness. It wouldn't be much of a surprise if the Brewers were aggressive with his promotions and put him on a fast track.

Variance: Low. There's still some talk of Ashby ending up in the bullpen, but the org is high on him, and it's likely he contributes soon, one way or another.

J.P. Breen's Fantasy Take: Plenty of minor-league pitchers can post gaudy strikeout numbers. When the strikeouts are paired with a high walk rate—his 2019 walk rate was north of 11 percent at both Class-A and High-A—it's a tough needle to thread. Ashby might be better in a multi-inning relief role, too, though the WHIP might not be good enough to make him valuable in standard roto leagues. The next pitcher on this list profiles as the better dynasty gamble.

4 Ethan Small   LHP   OFP: 55   ETA: Mid to Late 2021
Born: 02/14/97   Age: 24   Bats: L   Throws: L   Height: 6'4"   Weight: 215
Origin: Round 1, 2019 Draft (#28 overall)

The Report: Alongside Ashby, Small was one of the standouts at the Brewers alternate site. He boasts a four pitch mix; a lively fastball that sits either side of 90, a mid 70s changeup with late fade, a solid curve, and a newly developed slider. The fastball velocity plays up a bit due to a deceptive delivery, and he has average command of all four pitches, occasionally better. He's not afraid to use every weapon he has to disrupt a hitter's timing, often varying the rhythm of his wind up or slightly changing his leg kick.

Development Track: Small added a slider to his arsenal earlier this year and he's already developed it into an out pitch rather than a get me over one, improving it a full grade since spring training. He spent his season enhancing his secondaries and turning the trio into average offerings with flashes of something more. The fastball is still the star of the show, but now that it's accompanied by multiple other options, Small's on track to break into a major league rotation. The true test comes once he starts facing higher levels, as he's not yet pitched above Low-A ball.

Variance: Medium. Now that his offspeed pitches are legit offerings he looks a lot like an actual major leaguer. He'll still have to prove he's just as effective in-game next season as he was at the alternate site.

J.P. Breen's Fantasy Take: While not an exciting dynasty piece in the long term, Small could generate some significant buzz by Summer 2021. His improved secondary offerings, plus the quality command, should allow him to carve up minor-league hitting. A bloated strikeout rate and a shiny ERA might make him one of the summer's hottest trading chips. Long term, though, we're not looking at someone with the upside of a top-50 fantasy starter, unless the command is impeccable or the fastball adds a few ticks. Still, he's worth adding in deep dynasty leagues.

5. Mario Feliciano   C   OFP: 50   ETA: 2022
Born: 11/20/98   Age: 22   Bats: R   Throws: R   Height: 6'1"   Weight: 200
Origin: Round 2, 2016 Draft (#75 overall)

The Report: Feliciano exploded offensively at the alternate site. The potential with the bat has always been there, and he fully tapped into it this year. The contact rate is up, as his overall bat to ball skills have really come along and he's refined his approach at the plate. He sends hard line drives deep to all fields and has arguably the most power on the top ten.

Development Track: His ability to catch isn't quite the question mark it once was, but there's definitely still room for improvement. Currently the catching skills are just passable, good enough to get the job done with flashes of something more every so often. The strength of his arm is his best asset behind the dish and there's enough pure athleticism to ensure he remains at least average defensively. Feliciano's a bat-first backstop with the possibility of providing impact on both sides of the ball as long as he keeps making steady progress with the glove.

Variance: Medium. His offensive production is here to stay, but he's a catcher who still needs to improve defensively. The bat carries the profile.

J.P. Breen's Fantasy Take: Although I'm not allowed to advocate for dynasty catchers, other than one or two elite prospects, Feliciano has been one of my personal favorites for several years. Still, I'm not allowed to tell you to roster him. Mark Barry will yell at me.

6. Tristen Lutz   OF   OFP: 50   ETA: 2022
Born: 08/22/98   Age: 22   Bats: R   Throws: R   Height: 6'2"   Weight: 210
Origin: Round 1, 2017 Draft (#34 overall)

The Report: Completely filled out, Lutz is strong and athletic despite his large frame.

Likewise, he runs better than one might think, both on the base paths and in the field. He is destined to make the move to right field at some point. Lutz has the speed and the range to handle center, but he's a big guy with a strong accurate arm who's overall better suited for a corner spot. Defensively he's above average across the board, with power at the plate to match.

Development Track: Lutz's biggest hurdle is difficulty making consistent solid contact. When he gets the barrel on the ball he can hit it hard to every part of the park, plus game pop, even more raw power, but the hit tool just isn't where you want it to be. He's made some steps in the right direction this year, taking better swings and making mechanical adjustments, and also benefiting from daily at-bats against skilled arms at the alternate site. Whether or not he reaches his true ceiling relies heavily on him continuing to make contact and really showing off his plus power. He's slipped down the ranks, but he still has the potential to be a real difference maker.

Variance: Medium. Contact issues still plague Lutz, but he's made decent progress and his other tools are impressive enough to relieve some previous risk.

J.P. Breen's Fantasy Take: The raw power makes Lutz worth monitoring; however, he hasn't posted a .200 ISO in full-season ball and projects to be a drag in terms of batting average. To me, Lutz feels like Brandon Marsh with more questions about his hit tool. That's a hard pass from me for the moment, at least until we see tangible evidence of positive development at the plate.

7 Antoine Kelly   LHP   OFP: 50   ETA: Late-2022
Born: 12/05/99   Age: 21   Bats: L   Throws: L   Height: 6'6"   Weight: 205
Origin: Round 2, 2019 Draft (#65 overall)

The Report: A big JuCo popup arm from the 2019 Draft as a lefty who could touch triple digits, Kelly has developed well since getting into pro ball. He sits in the mid-90s with the fastball and it's free and easy heat. His slider projects as above-average to plus, and his changeup is coming along too. Kelly has had issues with his command—he's just a year off walking over 5 batters per 9 in the Great Rivers Athletic Conference, after all—but he seems to be putting things together ahead of schedule.

Development Track: Kelly gained valuable experience at the alternate site against more experienced hitters, working on his command and changeup. It's not clear to us that the alternate site and instructional league format was actually worse for starting pitchers than a normal season, given that it was much more controlled and it's not like pitching prospects throw 180 innings anyway.

Variance: High. He's got three innings of official game action above the complex level. The envelope of outcomes is quite high here, including ones where he's a lot better than a No. 4 starter. Full-season ball will be quite telling.

J.P. Breen's Fantasy Take: Kelly may not be a prep draftee, but it's not incorrect to treat him like one in terms of dynasty. He's one of several dozen interesting young arms in the complex leagues, but he has far too many questions about his command and his changeup to be worth rostering at the moment.

8. Freddy Zamora   SS   OFP: 50   ETA: 2023/2024
Born: 11/01/98   Age: 22   Bats: R   Throws: R   Height: 6'1"   Weight: 190
Origin: Round 2, 2020 Draft (#53 overall)

The Report: A collegiate shortstop who was among those with a big "arrow up" heading into this past Spring, Zamora didn't see the field at all after tearing his ACL in the pre-season. His reputation as a glove-first infielder with quick reactions, solid arm, and good body control were never in question. They were fully on display during his first two years at The U. Scouts wanted to see if he could begin driving the ball with more authority, having maintained decent batting averages and never striking out more than he walked. Signs of more power appeared to be in the cards following his sophomore season; even so, a plus defender with a solid eye at the plate and above-average contact rates would be worth a second round selection even with the injury.

Development Track: Torn knee ligaments aren't necessarily a career-altering injury thanks to modern medicine. But for a player whose skills are reliant upon fluid movements, it is a little more of a concern. Even if Zamora had a full, healthy junior year, there were going to be concerns to quell about the profile. You'd have liked to see more offensive development with more hard-hit contact, more muscle on his frame. Now we just need to see him fully rehabbed and on the field at all.

Variance: High. The good news is the variance is high because there is a far better chance he becomes a 55 rather than a 45. Playing a premium position and being more than capable defensively gets you pretty far on its own. His offensive value will determine his overall potential.

J.P. Breen's Fantasy Take: If you're getting Brice Turang vibes and aren't too excited about it, you're not alone. That might say more about Turang's fantasy upside than Zamora's, though. The injury adds more uncertainty. Don't worry about the former Cane until we see some professional reps.

9. Carlos Rodriguez   OF   OFP: 50   ETA: 2023/2024
Born: 12/07/00   Age: 20   Bats: L   Throws: L   Height: 5'10"   Weight: 150
Origin: International Free Agent, 2017

The Report: Rodriguez doesn't have the physicality or projection of your typical seven-figure IFA outfielder. What he has done is hit every place he's played in an admittedly brief pro career. Even here his profile confounds further, his .300+ batting averages don't originate from a typical "pretty" lefty swing. Rodriguez's mechanics are unorthodox, with an awkward, poking leg kick for timing.

Obviously it hasn't been an issue so far; he stays back well and the upper body works just fine. But it's definitely something you'd want to see work against better competition, which wasn't going to happen for him in 2020. And he'll need to hit: The lack of physicality and projection mean below-average power at best, and while he has the range for center field, we need to see more reps there as well.

Development Track: As you see throughout this list, the Brewers were extremely aggressive with assigning prospects—even low-level ones—to their alternate site. Rodriguez at least had a year of stateside reps before heading to Grand Chute this Summer, and it will be interesting to see if the Brewers considered his work there equivalent to significant A-ball reps. He'll spend all of next season as a 20-year-old, so "holding him back" in the Carolina League (gonna have to get used to this) wouldn't be all that conservative an assignment.

Variance: Extreme. This report may read as somewhat muted for a Top Ten outfield prospect, and sure, Milwaukee isn't the best or deepest system. But I do actually really like Rodriguez quite a bit. I think he'll hit, and I think there's positive variance here once we see that bat at higher levels. Sure, the swing isn't gonna end up hanging in the Louvre, but I find it pleasingly similar to the alien beauty of, like, Charline von Heyl.

J.P. Breen's Fantasy Take: Think Gilberto Jimenez (Red Sox) with a little better hit tool and slightly worse speed. He'll have to hit .300-plus for him to be an everyday guy. He has a legit chance to do that, though, and it's a good sign that the Brewers have continuously been aggressive with his assignments. Just remember that the best-case scenario is, like, Ender Inciarte—who is a nice little player but is easily replaceable in fantasy.

10 Hedbert Perez OF   OFP: 50   ETA: 2025ish
Born: 04/04/03   Age: 18   Bats: L   Throws: L   Height: 5'10"   Weight: 160
Origin: International Free Agent, 2019

The Report: Two years after signing Rodriguez out of Venezuela for a little over a million dollars, the Brewers inked Perez for $700,000. Perez has much more present strength and enough pop to generate good bat speed and loft from a fairly simple swing path, but both are advanced hitters for their age and experience level with a broad base of tools, even if they won't be sharing a wardrobe anytime soon. Or a position, as the barrel-chested Perez is likely destined for a corner outfield spot. He might well have the above-average hit and power tools to fit the profile.

Development Track: Perez was one of several high-profile 2019 J2s to get alternate site invites. We'd describe his performance as "buzzy." Buzzy enough to get him sent to a full-season affiliate for his 18th birthday? It's not impossible. I'm guessing he won't be the 10th best prospect in the Brewers system for 2022. And I'm guessing he won't be lower. But until he gets game reps, I am guessing more than I generally prefer.

Variance: Extreme. In a prospect list soaked with high variance profiles, Perez hasn't played an official game yet and doesn't turn 18 until Opening Day 2021.

J.P. Breen's Fantasy Take: Given Perez's post-J2 buzz, it's unlikely that he's available in deeper dynasty leagues. And very little has changed over the past 12 months. He's an intriguing young hitter who could potentially produce in terms of average and power. We just have very little on which to go, outside of a few buzzy reports. With that said, I won't blame you for rolling the dice in a deep dynasty, if he's available in your league.

The Prospects You Meet Outside The Top Ten

Zavier Warren   Born: 01/08/99   Age: 22   Bats: S   Throws: R   Height: 6'0"   Weight: 190   Origin: Round 3, 2020 Draft (#92 overall)

The ultimate baseball swiss-army knife—a player who can play any position-- Warren bounced all over the diamond during his college career, getting the bulk of his starts at shortstop. He has the arm strength to throw out runners from behind the plate, or from the 6-hole, or across the diamond at third base; it's possible his value is derived from not having a clear defensive home. He's also a capable switch-hitter with the ability to spray line-drives from foul line to foul line thanks to short, compact swing that is a little better from the left side, where the bat speed and swing plane are more evident, not that his right-handed stroke is that far off.

Eduardo Garcia   SS   Born: 07/10/02   Age: 18   Bats: R   Throws: R   Height: 6'2"   Weight: 160   Origin: International Free Agent, 2019

Milwaukee's big IFA signing of 2018 checks in just outside the top ten after a fractured ankle cut short his time in the Dominican complex last Summer. It's a broadly similar profile to Zamora, right down to the recent bad leg injury. Garcia is a potential plus shortstop whose offensive tools lag behind the glove, but there's enough of a chance that the bat gets to average that the ordinal gap between them on this list overstates the projection gap. Honestly you could put 5-12 in this system in almost any permutation depending on your risk tolerance and profile preference.

Top Talents 25 and Under (as of 4/1/2021):

1. Keston Hiura, 2B
2. Brice Turang, SS
3. Garrett Mitchell, OF
4. Freddy Peralta, RHP

5. Luis Urías, IF
6. Aaron Ashby, LHP
7. Ethan Small, LHP
8. Mario Feliciano, C
9. Tristen Lutz, OF
10. Eric Lauer, LHP

Well, it gets a little better down here, I suppose. Keston Hiura never really got going in 2020, striking out nearly 35 percent of the time and hitting the ball an average of 4 MPH softer when he did hit it. Despite that, he was still close to a league-average hitter (98 DRC+), and we're extremely confident in the underlying hitting ability that made him the No. 6 prospect in baseball two years ago and drove his big 2019 rookie campaign.

Freddy Peralta has been a whiff machine for the Brewers, mostly out of the bullpen. He's virtually eliminated his changeup in favor of a new slider; there's only a handful of true fastball/slider/curveball starters around the league, so he might need to drop the occasional change in just for an armside look if he's going to slide back to the rotation. But there's nothing else really saying he can't at least be a twice through the order guy, and a lot of his relief appearances have already come in long relief. We'd like the Brewers to give it a shot.

Luis Urías was a top 25 prospect not that long ago based on a high-end hit tool projection, and now he's hit .226 over parts of three MLB seasons. He's not making as much contact as we thought he would and he's not hitting it all that hard when he does, which is a bad combo. The latent bat-to-ball is probably still there and he's a versatile defender, so we're not totally out, but his stock is slipping.

Eric Lauer was pretty awful this year coming off a trade from the Padres. In literally any other system, he wouldn't have made this list. But it's the Brewers and he looked like a No. 4 starter in 2019, so…

Part 3: Featured Articles

Brewers All-Time Top 10 Players

by Matthew Trueblood

POSITION PLAYERS

GEORGE SCOTT, 1B (1972-1976)
With some cause, Scott felt unappreciated and frustrated throughout his Milwaukee tenure. He (correctly, in all likelihood) felt that the organization and the fans were quick to point fingers at him when the team underachieved because he was Black. In truth, failing to keep Scott happy was the franchise's failure, and their struggles in those years weren't his fault. On the contrary, he won Gold Glove awards at first base in all five of his Brewers seasons, hit for power and average with his vicious right-handed swing, and was worth 26.1 WARP. Not many hitters leave Fenway Park and get better; "Boomer" was one of the few exceptions.

CECIL COOPER, 1B (1977-1987)
From the mid-1960s through the mid-1970s, the Red Sox were a well-oiled scouting and development machine, churning out a bevy of excellent hitters. In various ways, a few of them landed in and had great careers for the Brewers. Scott (above) was one of them. When the Brewers traded him back to Boston, they acquired the young, lithe, smooth-fielding Cooper. He hit as though cornered with a swing-happy approach, his back foot on the back line, and his front foot reaching for the far edge of the box, but it worked: he made tons of contact and hit for a high average. Once he found power, in 1979, he became one of the best first basemen in baseball. His career stats are almost identical to Don Mattingly's, but only one of them is mentioned as a Hall of Fame candidate.

JIM GANTNER, 2B (1976-1992)

The presence of Molitor and Yount on the left side of the infield and at the top of the batting order ensured that Gantner would spend his entire career at the keystone and at the bottom of the lineup. That wasn't such a bad fate, though. He was a slick fielder and a great singles hitter. He utterly lacked power and plate discipline, but he got on base in front of Molitor and Yount enough to become a valuable part of the team's offensive engine for over a decade. In short, he occupied an unusual space where he was far from being a star but also wasn't a problem.

DON MONEY, 3B (1973-1983)

When the Brewers first acquired Scott from Boston, they also got several other players, but a few of them were destined to be packaged and flipped to Philadelphia. That trade brought (among others) Money to Milwaukee, where he overcame a half-decade of inconsistency and frustration for the Phillies and became a four-time All-Star. He never posted gaudy numbers, but for his era and home park, he was a solid, patient, slugging hitter, and he played average-plus defense at the hot corner.

JEFF CIRILLO, 3B (1994-99, 2005-2006)

Unlike so many of his contemporaries, Cirillo was no power hitter. He derived almost all his value from a balanced, patient approach, a willingness to shorten up and use the opposite field, and his excellent defense at third base. That was a recipe for being overlooked much of the time, in part because of the quality of teams for which he played. Yet, Cirillo earned broad respect for his overall hitting skills, and for his leadership and clubhouse presence. His second stint with the club proved to be more than a nostalgic indulgence; he was still an above-average hitter and became a beloved veteran, cementing his legacy with the team and fans.

ROBIN YOUNT, SS/OF (1974-1993)

Nobody comes up at age 18 and thrives in the big leagues. It took Yount half a decade to blossom into a star, but he was still shy of age 25 when he did. Self-possessed and independent, he weathered early injury issues and once stayed away for the first month and a half of a season to contemplate whether he still wanted to play the game. He used an extremely unorthodox, closed stance with an odd grip on the bat. He found very good power in that style, ran the bases well, and was a great defender at shortstop until shoulder trouble forced him to the outfield. In baseball history, only Yount has played 1,000 or more games at both shortstop and center field. In fact, no one else has even played 400 at each spot. His 1982 MVP season (.331/.379/.578, 46 doubles, 12 triples, 29 home runs) is still one of the best any shortstop has ever had.

PAUL MOLITOR, 3B/DH/2B (1978-1992)

The Brewers moved "The Ignitor" all over the diamond, which wasn't as much about his defensive skills as just keeping him healthy. A decade into his career, they still hadn't really found a way to do that, but it didn't matter; Molitor was such a well-rounded offensive weapon that he really did thrive even as a nomadic fielder. He hit for average and gap power and stole bases both often and efficiently. His quiet, short swing and all-fields approach, plus his speed, made him a nightmare for defenders, and allowed him to age gracefully. The Brewers made Molitor the third overall pick of the 1977 draft. The two players who went before him, Harold Baines and Bill Gullickson, were pretty good too, but not at his level.

BEN OGILVIE, OF (1978-1986)

Yet another product of the Boston system in the 1960s, Oglivie spent a four-year interregnum in Detroit before landing with the Brewers. Like Rod Carew, he was born in Panama but moved to New York in his teens and was discovered there. He was a brilliant, reserved person, and a bit of a square peg in the round hole of a big-league clubhouse in the 1970s. Racism and biases bound up in the evaluation of Afro-Latino players led to too long a wait for regular playing time, but once he found it, he emerged as a star. High-waisted and upright in the batter's box, he cut loose a violent swing from a quiet, even stance. That produced 136 home runs in his first five years as a Brewer, and he also hit for average. In 1980, he became the first foreign-born player to lead either league in home runs. That season was something of an oddity in a career that was consistently inconsistent—in 1978 he hit a home run every 26 at-bats, in 1979 every 18, in 1980 every 14. In 1981 he was down to one every 29, then one every 18 in 1982 and one every 32 in 1983.

GEOFF JENKINS, OF (1998-2007)

The Brewers made Jenkins the ninth-overall pick of the 1995 draft. It was fun to watch him hit because every swing contained so much unguarded ambition: He wanted to hit the snot out of the ball. He employed a leg kick and would let his front foot hover a bit as a timing mechanism, then cut loose with everything he had. He was undisciplined and strikeout-prone but ran high BABIPs and could hit the ball out of any part of the park. While he wouldn't be around when the Brewers finally made it back to the playoffs—always prone to injury, his worse down early—he was a symbol of their ascendant offense in the years immediately preceding that breakthrough.

RYAN BRAUN, OF/3B (2007-2020)

Although Braun's comportment during the Biogenesis saga will always be part of his legacy, it would be folly to treat his career as a product of performance-enhancing drugs. Watching his swing—the high start of his hands, then the lightning-quick, slashing uppercut to a high finish to rival any sweet-swinging lefty—made his raw talent and dedication to the craft of hitting apparent. He was never especially patient at the plate, but he didn't trade contact for either exit velocity or launch angle as much as many sluggers do. He could drive the ball out of the park to right field, hit line drives from gap to gap, and run well enough (with two 30-30 seasons) to help the team on the bases. Another good draft pick by the Brewers (fifth overall in 2005's loaded first round), although his unsuitability for third base was still a lesson they had to learn the hard way in 2007.

PITCHERS

JIM SLATON, RHP (1971-1977, 1979-1983)

The all-time franchise leader in innings pitched might have made his greatest contribution to the team by being traded for Ben Oglivie. A year after that deal, he was a free agent, and the Brewers scooped him back up. His second stint was much less successful than his first: After pitching an average of 251 innings per year from 1973-1977, he wore down in his early 30s. A good slider became his only weapon, but he used it to generate enough mishits and called strikes to stay afloat for several more seasons.

JIM COLBORN, RHP (1972-1976)

Milwaukee was just a stop in Colborn's career as a journeyman innings eater, but it was certainly his best one. He threw 314 innings for the Crew in 1973 and totaled 1,118 in just five seasons with them. One mystery of the Brewers is how the team so consistently produced medium-sized right-handed guys who had average velocity, an average slider, and no third pitch to speak of for 20 solid years. It wasn't a recipe for any kind of run-prevention dominance, but it allowed their impressive hitters to lift them to contention on multiple occasions.

MOOSE HAAS, RHP (1976-1985)

Bryan's father hoped for a football player (hence the nickname), but Haas didn't grow to the right size for that. Instead, he took good overall athleticism and an average build to the mound, where he developed a good but not bat-missing slider, learned to elevate his tepid fastball effectively, and found feel for a changeup late in his career. Commanding the slider well and sinking the fastball more as he aged, he became slightly more effective and consistent even as he struck out fewer batters.

MIKE CALDWELL, LHP (1977-1984)

The granddaddy of the Brewers' pitch-to-contact cadre, Caldwell passed through four organizations before he was dumped on the Brewers for two players who never made the majors. He proved to be a steal. He filled up the strike zone from a low-three-quarters arm angle, sometimes even throwing sidearm, and was thus excelled at keeping the ball on the ground and in the ballpark. He managed contact well, giving him better results than modern metrics would predict. It was a different game. In 1978, Caldwell went 22-9 with a 2.36 ERA, pitched 23 complete games, and finished as the runner-up to Ron Guidry in Cy Young voting—although some suspected he managed that by throwing a wet sinker.

TEDDY HIGUERA, LHP (1985-1994)
Already 25 when the Brewers coaxed him away from the Mexican League, Higuera was 27 when he debuted. That made for a short peak, especially because back, ankle, and shoulder trouble quickly derailed him. While he was healthy, however, he was both dominant and delightful. With a quick, high-kicking, angular delivery, he gave hitters a rollercoaster ride: First a high fastball, then a curve that buckled the knees or drew a lurching flail of a swing. From 1986-88, he was worth 16.7 WARP. If you could choose any pitcher in Brewers history to start that one big game, Higuera would be the consensus choice.

BILL WEGMAN, RHP (1985-1995)
When he was healthy enough to pitch at all, Wegman held the mound like it was the Alamo. Tall but not hard-throwing, he became dependent upon throwing his slider for strikes and minimizing damage. After arm trouble truncated both his 1989 and 1990 seasons, he still averaged over seven innings per start in 1991 and 1992. He pounded the strike zone relentlessly but didn't miss bats and gave up home runs at a high rate.

CHRIS BOSIO, RHP (1986-1992)
A pugnacious, portly right-hander, Bosio went right after hitters. He lacked the stuff to miss bats (a theme, sometimes to hilarious extremes, for the Brewers), but filled up the zone and changed speeds constantly. Like several other Brewers starters who pitched just before or alongside him, he was a workhorse, sometimes at the expense of his best possible performance. He came up as a swingman, but once he claimed a full-time starting role, he accrued 14.4 WARP in four years before leaving for the Mariners.

CAL ELDRED, RHP (1991-1999)
Strapping and imposing, former first-rounder Eldred briefly emerged as a true workhorse for some bad Brewers teams. In 1993 and 1994, he made 61 total starts, leading the majors. He pitched 258 innings in the former season and was on almost the same pace before the labor wars truncated the latter. Not entirely coincidentally, he underwent Tommy John surgery early the following year and

was never the same. His smooth, old-fashioned delivery (with the hands going behind his head on each windup) kept him around the zone and in the league for another fistful of seasons.

BEN SHEETS, RHP (2001-2008)

In 2004, Sheets had one of the great seasons by a starting pitcher in the 21st century. He fanned 264 batters and walked just 32, in 238 innings. The flame-throwing Louisiana native, selected 10th overall in the first round of the 1999 draft, was profoundly unlike almost every other good pitcher in Milwaukee history. He overpowered opponents. Injuries took their toll after high innings totals early in his career, but he amassed 36.1 WARP in fewer than 1,509 innings with the Crew.

YOVANI GALLARDO, RHP (2007-2014)

A rookie phenom in 2007, Gallardo was the ace of the Brewers as they awoke from a decade and a half of competitive slumber. After a bad knee injury in 2008, he didn't throw exceptionally hard but retained an over-the-top arm angle that gave him an excellent movement profile. His fastball had some of the best carry in the big leagues, with very little run to the arm side. That made both his slider and his curveball, with tons of depth but little sweeping action, especially deceptive. He hit well too—in 2010 he averaged .254/.329/.508 with four home runs.

A Taxonomy of 2020 Abnormalities

by Rob Mains

I'm going to start this with a trivia question. Trust me, it's relevant. Don't bother skipping to the end of the article to find the answer, it's not there.

Only five players have appeared in 140 or more games for 16 straight seasons. Who are they?

It's a trivia question starting off an essay, so you know how this works: Whatever you guessed, you're wrong. It's okay. As someone who purchased this book, chances are good that you're an educated baseball fan. But the circumstances behind 2020 force us to abandon, or at least seriously question, some of our favorite patterns and crutches for evaluating the game we love.

We just completed what was undoubtedly the strangest season in MLB history. No fans, geographically limited schedule, universal DH, seven-inning twin bills, runners on second in extra innings, a 16-team postseason, a club playing at a Triple-A stadium. Some of these changes will likely persist (sorry), but we've never had so many tweaks dumped on us all at once, at least not since they figured out how many balls were in a walk.

And the biggest, of course, was the 60-game season. The 19th century was dotted with teams that went bankrupt before the season ended, but the lone season with only 60 scheduled games was 1877. That year there were only six teams, the league rostered a total of 77 players (just 16 more than the 2020 Marlins), and batters called for pitches to be thrown high or low by the pitcher, who was 50 feet away. We can say the 2020 season was easily the shortest ever for recognizable baseball.

As such, it'll stand out. Few abbreviated seasons do. Just about everybody reading this knows the 1994 season ended after Seattle's Randy Johnson struck out Oakland's Ernie Young for the last out of the Mariners-A's game on August 11. The ensuing player strike wiped out the rest of the season and the postseason. Teams played only 112-117 games that year.

And many of you know that a strike in the middle of the 1981 season split the season in two, resulting in the only Division Series until 1995. Teams played only 103-111 games that year, the shortest regular season since 1885.

Those two seasons are memorable. So when we see that nobody drove in 100 runs in 1981, or that Greg Maddux was the only pitcher with 180 or more innings pitched in 1994, we think, "Of course. Strike year."

But we don't remember other short years. You might not recall that the 1994 strike spilled into the next year, chopping 18 games off the 1995 schedule. You might've read that the 1918 season, played during the last pandemic, ended after Labor Day due to the government's World War I "work or fight" order. A strike erased the first week and a half of the 1972 season, but that year's best known as the last time pitchers batted in the American League.

The point is, while we don't remember small changes to the schedule, we remember the big ones. The 1981 mid-season strike. The 1994 season- and Series-ending strike. And, of course, the pandemic-shortened 2020 season. We won't need a reminder why Marcell Ozuna's 18 homers were the fewest to lead the National League in a century. (Literally; Cy Williams led with 15 in 1920.)

Now, about that trivia question. The five players are Hank Aaron, Brooks Robinson, Pete Rose, Ichiro Suzuki, and Johnny Damon. The one nobody gets, of course, is Damon, and a lot of people miss Ichiro, whose last season of 140-plus games came garbed in the red-orange and ocean blue of Miami when he was 42. That's half of what makes it a good question. The other half is the two guys whom many think made the list but didn't. Lou Gehrig? His streak started in the Yankees' 42nd game of the 1925 season and lasted only 13 seasons after that. And everybody assumes Cal Ripken Jr. did it, having played 2,632 straight games over 17 seasons. But one of those 17 seasons was 1994, when the Orioles played only 112 games.

My point? *I just told you* everybody remembers the 1994 strike year, but everybody forgets it fell in the middle of Ripken's streak, separating the first twelve years from the last four. Just because we recall something doesn't mean it's always at the front of our minds.

Nobody is going to forget 2020, and baseball is obviously not the main reason. But there will come a time in the future when you're looking at a player's or a team's record, and there will be baffling numbers there for 2020, and you'll think, "I wonder what happened." (Not to mention the missing line for minor league players.) Just like you forgot that the 1994 strike limited Ripken to 112 games.

Try not to forget it, though. The 2020 season resulted in weird statistical results for several reasons.

There were only 60 games.

I know, duh. But that had impacts beyond counting stats like Ozuna's home run total or Yu Darvish and Shane Bieber leading the majors with eight wins. (I know, pitcher wins, but still.)

The 162-game season is the longest among major North American sports, and that duration gives us a gift. Over the course of a long season, small variations tend to even out. A player who has a ten-game hot streak will probably have a ten-game cold streak. A team that starts the year losing a bunch of close games will probably win a bunch of them. We get regression to the mean. Statistics stabilize.

Consider flipping a coin. Over the long run, we expect it to come up heads about half the time. But the fewer flips, the more variation there'll be. If you flip a coin six times, probability theory tells us you'll get at least two-third heads about 34 percent of the time. Flip it 30 times, your chance of two-thirds heads drops to five percent.

Or, relevant to this case, if you flip a coin 60 times, your chance of getting at least 36 heads—that's 60 percent—is 7.75 percent. Expand the coin-flipping to 162 times, and the chance of getting 60 percent heads drops to 0.73 percent.

In other words, the odds of an outcome that's 20 percent better (or worse) than expected is *more than ten times higher* when you flip your coin 60 times than when you do it 162 times. Call it small sample size, call lack of mean reversion, or call it luck not evening out, 162 is a lot more predictive than 60. You get much more variation over 60 games than over 162. Bieber's 1.63 ERA and 0.87 FIP aren't something we'd see over a full season, and neither is Javier Baéz's .203/.238/.360.

Some players' lines in 2020 look normal. Brian Anderson had an .811 OPS in 2019 and an .810 OPS in 2020. (He probably would have gotten that last point if he'd been given enough time.) But there are many like Bieber and Baéz, some of them from young players still establishing their talent levels. The answer to the question, "What went right or wrong for that guy in 2020?" is most likely "Nothing, it was just a 2020 thing."

Preseason training was abbreviated for hitters.

Every year, spring training drags. Players get tired of it, fans get tired of it, and you sure can tell sportswriters get tired of it. Yes, something to get everyone into shape is necessary, but does it really have to drag on for over a month? Can't we shorten it?

The 2020 season answered in the negative, at least for hitters. Warren Spahn is credited with saying that hitting is timing and pitching is upsetting timing. It appears nobody had his timing down after the abbreviated July summer camp. Through August 9—18 games into the season—MLB batters were hitting .230/.311/.395 with a .275 BABIP. That BABIP, had it held, would have been the lowest since 1968, the Year of the Pitcher. In recent years it's hovered around .300.

It didn't hold. Play returned to more normal levels the rest of the year: .249/.325/.425 with a .297 BABIP starting August 10. But batters whose play concentrated in those first two weeks wound up with ugly lines. Andrew

Benintendi went on the injured list with a season-ending rib cage strain on August 11. His final line: .103/.314/.128 in 14 games. Franchy Cordero went on the IL with a hamate bone fracture on August 9 and a .154/.185/.231 line. Even though he came back strong in a late September return, it was too late to repair his full-season numbers.

Preseason training was abbreviated for pitchers.

Every year, spring training drags. Players get tired of it, fans get tired of it ... wait, I already said that. But the abbreviated preseason was tough on pitchers, too. As noted, they had the upper hand coming out of the gate. But then they lost that hand. And then their arms, too.

The 2020 season was spread over 67 days. During those 67 days, 237 pitchers hit the Injured List, compared to 135 in the first 67 days of 2019. A lot of those IL stints, though, were COVID-19-related. Still, over the first 67 days of the 2019 season, there were 72 pitchers on the IL with arm injuries. That figure jumped to 110 in 2020, a 53 percent increase.

There are a number of factors contributing to pitcher arm injuries, ranging from usage to velocity, but it appears that attenuated preseason training played a role. A lot of pitchers had super-short seasons due to arm woes. Corey Kluber, Roberto Osuna, and Shohei Ohtani combined for seven innings, none after August 8. All suffered arm injuries. We'll never know whether they'd have fared better with a longer preseason, but we can guess how they probably feel.

Everybody played.

Rosters were set to expand from 25 to 26 in 2020, so even if we'd had a normal season, we'd have likely seen 2019's record of 1,410 players on MLB rosters broken. But due to the pandemic, rosters started the year at 30 and were cut to only 28. Add multiple COVID-19 absences and the revolving door caused by poor starts by hitters and a rash of pitcher arm injuries, and 1,289 players appeared in MLB games in 2020. The comparable figure over the first 67 days of the 2019 season was 1,109. That 16 percent increase works out to an average of six more players per team in 2020 compared to a similar slice of 2019. A future look back at 2020 rosters will include a lot of unfamiliar names.

Plus became a minus.

In advanced metrics, we adjust batter and pitcher performance for park and league/era variations. A plus sign appended to the end of a measure means that it's adjusted for park and league. It's scaled to an average of 100, with higher figures above average and lower figures below average. (Similarly, a metric with a minus is also park- and league-adjusted and scaled to 100, with lower values better.) Here at BP, our advanced measure of offensive performance is DRC+. Baseball-Reference has OPS+ and FanGraphs has wRC+.

Using park and league adjustments, we can compare Dante Bichette's 1995 Steroid Era season at pre-humidor Coors Field (.340/.364/.620, 40 homers, 128 RBI, MVP runner-up) with Jim Wynn's 1968 Year of the Pitcher season at the cavernous Astrodome (.269/.376/.474, 26 homers, 67 RBI, no MVP votes). It's not close. DRC+, OPS+, and wRC+ all give the nod to Wynn, handily. This is a useful tool. As my Baseball Prospectus colleague Patrick Dubuque tweeted last fall, "Please note that when I ask how you are, I am already adjusting for era."

The 2020 season messes up plus (and minus) stats for two reasons. First, the park adjustment was based on only 30 home games instead of the usual 81. Everything noted above regarding the short season applies, literally doubly, to park effect calculations. DRC+ uses a single-season park factor. OPS+ uses a three-year average and wRC+ five years. The figure for 2020 is suspect.

Second, OPS+ and wRC+ adjust for league: American and National. (DRC+ adjusts for opponent, regardless of league.) While there were two leagues in 2020, they were an artificial construct. To reduce travel, teams played opponents geographically, not based on league. There weren't two leagues, American and National. There were three, Western, Central, and Eastern.

That makes a difference because teams in the same league played in different run-scoring environments. AL teams scored 4.58 runs per game, NL teams 4.71. That's a small difference. But teams in the East scored 0.21 more runs per game (4.95) than teams in the West (4.74), and they both scored a lot more than Central teams (4.25). Adjusting for league misses that difference, so this book will be safe in that regard, but other sources may be distorted somewhat.

Not every game was a "game."
In 2020, the rising tide of strikeouts was finally stemmed. Strikeouts per team per game fell from 8.8 in 2019 to 8.7 in 2020. That marked the first decline after 14 straight annual increases.

In 2020, the rising tide of strikeouts rose higher. Batters struck out in 23.4 percent of plate appearances compared to 23.0 percent in 2019. That marked the 15th straight annual increase.

Both are true statements.

Because of two rule changes—seven-inning doubleheaders and runners on second in extra innings—games in 2020 were unprecedented in their brevity. There were 37.0 plate appearances per game in 2020. The only years with fewer were 1904 and 1906-1909. The average game in 2020 entailed 8.61 innings pitched, the fewest since 1899.

So when you see any per-game stats for 2020, you need to increase them by 3 or 4 percent to get them on equal footing with recent years.

Or, better, just ignore them. Last year happened. There were major league games contested between major league teams. But when you're looking at those physical or electronic baseball cards, when you're weaving narratives over why this young player's inevitable rise to stardom fell apart or why that old veteran rekindled his magic, don't linger on the 2020 line. It was just too weird.

Thanks to Lucas Apostoleris for research assistance.

—Rob Mains is an author of Baseball Prospectus.

Tranches of WAR

by Russell A. Carleton

We ask "replacement level" to be a lot of things. Sometimes contradictory things. Sometimes I wonder if we know what it even means anymore. The original idea was that it represented the level of production that a team could expect to get from "freely available talent", including bench players, minor leaguers, and waiver wire pickups. It created a common benchmark to compare everyone to, and for that reason, it represented an advancement well beyond what was available at the time. In fact, it created a language and a framework for evaluating players that was not just better but *entirely* different than what came before it.

But then we started mumbling in that language. The idea behind "wins above replacement" was one part sci-fi episode and one part mathematical exercise. Imagine that a player had disappeared before the season and suddenly, in an alternate timeline, his team would have had to replace him. The distance between him and that replacement line was his value. We need to talk about that alternate timeline.

Without getting too into 2:00 am "deep conversations" with extensive navel-gazing, it's worth thinking about why one player might not be playing, while another might.

- A player might not be playing because he has a short-term injury or his manager believes that he needs a day off.
- A player might not be playing because he has a longer-term injury that requires him to be on the injured list.

There's a difference here between these two situations. In particular, the first one generally *doesn't* involve a compensatory roster move, while the second one does. It's possible, though not guaranteed, that the person who will be replacing the injured/resting player would be the same in either case. That matters. Teams generally carry a spare part for all eight position players on the diamond, although in the era of a four-player bench, those spare parts usually are the backup plan for more than one spot.

A couple of years ago, I posed a hypothetical question. Suppose that a team had two players in its system fighting for a fourth outfielder spot. One of them was a league average hitter, but would be worth 20 runs below average if allowed to play center field for a full season. One of them was a perfectly average fielder, but would be 15 runs below average as a hitter, if allowed to play an entire season. Which of the two should the team roster? It's tempting to say the second one, as overall, he is the better player. That misses the point. A league average hitter on the bench isn't just a potential replacement for an injured outfielder. He might also pinch hit for the light-hitting shortstop in a key spot. You keep the average hitter on the roster, even though he isn't a hand-in-glove fit for one specific place on the field, because being a bench player is a different job description than being a long-term fill-in for someone. If you find yourself in need of a longer-term fill-in, you can bring the other guy up from AAA.

When we're determining the value of an everyday player though, if he had disappeared before the season and a team would have had to replace his production, they likely would have done it with a player who was a long-term fill-in type because they would have had to replace a guy who played everyday. Maybe that's the same guy that they would have rostered on their bench anyway, but we don't know. It gets to the query of what we hope to accomplish with WAR. Are we looking for an accurate modeling of reality or are we looking for a common baseline to compare everyone to? Both have their uses, but they are somewhat different questions.

Let's talk about another dichotomy.

- A player might not be playing because he isn't very good and is a bench-level player.
- A player might not be playing because there is another player on the team who has a situational advantage that makes him the better choice today. The classic case of this is a handedness platoon. On another day, he might be a better choice.

When we think about player usage, I think we're still stuck in the model that there are starters and there are scrubs. We have plenty of words for bench players or reserves or backups or utility guys. We do still have the word "platoon" in our collective vocabulary, but in the age of short benches, it's hard to construct one. It's always been hard to construct them. You have to find two players who hit with different hands, have skill sets that complement each other, and probably play the same position. In the era of the short bench, one of them had probably better double as a utility player in some way. Baseball has a two-tiered language geared toward the idea of regulars and reserves. The fact that it was so easy for me to find plenty of synonyms for "a player whose primary function is to come into a game to replace a regular player if he is injured or resting" should tell you something.

I'm always one to look for "unspoken words" in baseball. What is it called when someone is both half of a platoon and the utility infielder? That guy exists sometimes, but he reveals himself in that role—usually by accident. We don't have a word for that, and whenever I find myself saying "we don't have a word for that", I look for new opportunities. What do you call it, further, when the job of being the utility infielder is decentralized across the whole infield with occasional contributions from the left fielder? It's not even a "super-utility" player. What happens when you build your entire roster around the idea that everyone will be expected to be a triple major?

⚾ ⚾ ⚾

I think someone else beat me to this one, and on a grand scale. Platoons work because we know that hitters of the opposite hand to the pitcher get better results than hitters of the same hand, usually to the tune of about 20 points of OBP. If you want to express that in runs, it usually comes out to somewhere around 10 to 12 runs of linear weights value prorated across 650 PA. But hang on a second, now let's say that we have two players who might start today, both of roughly equal merit with the bat. One has a handedness advantage, but is the worse fielder of the two. In that case, as long as his "over the course of a season" projection as a fielder at whatever position you want to slot him into is less than a 10-run drop from the guy he might replace, then he's a better option today.

We're not used to thinking of utility players as bat-first options, who would play below-average defense at three different infield positions. That guy might hook on as a 2B/3B/LF type (Howie Kendrick, come on down!) but teams usually think to themselves that they need as their utility infielder someone who "can handle" shortstop, the toughest of the infield spots to play. If someone can do that *and* hit well, he's probably already starting somewhere, so he's not available as a utility infielder. It's easier for those glove guys to find a job. In a world where the replacement for a shortstop *has to be* the designated utility infielder, that makes sense.

But as we talked about last week, we're living in a different world. The rate at which a replacement for a regular starter turns out to be *another starter* shifting over to cover has gone way up over the last five years. There was always some of it in the game, but this has been a supernova of switcheroos. Now if your second baseman is capable of playing a decent shortstop, that 2B/3B/LF guy can swap in. He's not actually playing shortstop, and maybe the defense suffers from the switch, but if he's got enough of a bat, he might outhit those extra fielding miscues. And in doing so, he is effectively your backup shortstop.

Somewhere along the lines, teams got hip to the idea of multi-positional play from their regulars. I've written before about how you can't just put a player, however athletic, into a new position and expect much at first. The data tell us that. Eventually, players can learn to be multi-positionalists, but it takes time, roughly on the order of two months, before they're OK. But there's a hidden message in there. If you give a player some reps at a new spot, he's a reasonably gifted athlete and somewhat smart and willing to learn, he could probably pick it up enough to get to "good enough," and it doesn't take forever. You just have to be purposeful about it. Maybe you get to the point where you can start to say "he's still below average but we could move him there and get another bat into the lineup, and it's a net win."

Teams have started to build those extra lessons into their player development program. It used to be seen as a mark of weakness to be relegated to "utility player" because that meant that you were a bench player (all those synonyms above come with a side of stigma). Now, it's a way of building a team. If you get a few reps in the minors (where it doesn't count) at a spot, you'll have at least played the spot at game speed before. There are limits to how far you can push that. A slow-footed "he's out in left field because we don't have the DH" guy is never going to play short, but maybe your third baseman can try second base and not look like a total moose out there.

⚾ ⚾ ⚾

Back to WAR. I'd argue that the world of starters and scrubs is slowly disintegrating, for good cause. In the event that a regular starter really does go down with an injury–ostensibly, the alternate universe scenario that WAR is attempting to model–it makes the team a little more resilient to replacing him. And the good news is that you're more likely to be able to replace him with the best of the bench bunch, rather than the third-best guy, because the best guy doesn't have to be an exact positional match for the guy who got hurt. And that's what the manager would want to do. He'd want to replace that long-term production, not with an amalgam of everyone else who played that position, but with the best guy available from his reserves.

Now this is still WAR. We still want to retain the principle that we should be measuring a player, and not his teammates. We need some sort of common baseline, and despite what I just said, we'll still need some sort of amalgam. To construct that, I give to you the idea of the tranche. The word, if you've not heard it before, refers to a piece of a whole that is somehow segmented off. It's often used in finance to talk about layers of a financial instrument.

Here, I want you to consider that there are 30 starters at each of the seven non-battery positions (catchers should have their own WAR, since only a catcher can replace a catcher). We can identify them by playing time, and we can futz around with the definition a little bit if we need to. Next, among those who aren't in that starting pool, we identify the top tranche of the 30 best bench players, which I would again identify by playing time, and then the second and third and fourth and so on. If a player were to disappear, his manager would probably want to take a guy from that top tranche of the bench to replace him. In a world where even the starters can slide around the field, that becomes more feasible.

We can take a look at that top tranche and say "How many of them showed that they are able to play (first, second, etc.)?" and therefore could have directly substituted for the starter? How many of them could have been a direct substitute for our injured player? We don't know whether one of them would be on *a specific* team, but we can say that 40 percent of the time, a manager would have been able to draw from tranche 1 in filling the role, and 35 percent from tranche 2. But on tranche 1, we can also look at how many of those players played a position that could have then shifted and covered for that spot. We'd need some eligibility criteria for all of this (probably a minimum number of games played) but it would just be a matter of multiplication. Shortstop would be harder to fill, and managers would probably be dipping a little further down in the talent pool, and so replacement level would be lower, as it is now.

Doing some quick analysis, I found that the difference in just batting linear weights (haven't even gotten into running or fielding) between tranche 1 and tranche 2 in 2019 was about 6.5 runs, prorated across 650 PA. Between tranche 1 and tranche 3, it's 10.8 runs. The ability to shift those plate appearances up the ladder has some real value.

This part is important. We can also give credit to starters for the positions that they showed an ability to play, even if they didn't play them (this is the guy fully capable of playing center, but who's in a corner because the team already has a good center fielder) because he allows a team to carry a player who hits like a left fielder to functionally be the team's backup center fielder. He facilitates that movement upward among the tranches. We can start to appreciate the difference between a left fielder who would never be able to hack it in center (and the compensatory move that his team would have to make) and the left fielder who could do it, but just didn't have to very often.

Past that, you can continue to use whatever hitting and fielding and running metrics you like to determine a player's value, but when we get down to constructing that baseline, I'd argue we need a better conceptual and mathematical framework. It's going to require some more #GoryMath than we're used to, but I'd argue it's a better conceptualization of the way that MLB actually plays the game in 2020. If…y'know…MLB plays in 2020. If WAR is going to be our flagship statistic among the *acronymati*, then we need to acknowledge that it contains some old and starting-to-be-out-of-date assumptions about the game. We may need to tinker with it. Here's my idea for how.

—*Russell A. Carleton is an author of Baseball Prospectus.*

Secondhand Sport

by Patrick Dubuque

Back before time stopped, I liked to go to thrift stores. Now that I'm older, I rarely ever buy anything—I don't need much in my life, now—but I still enjoy the old familiar circuit: check to see if there are baseball cards to write about, look for board or card games to play with the kids, scan for random ironic jerseys, hit the book section. It takes ten, maybe fifteen minutes. Thrift stores are the antithesis of modern online shopping, because you don't know what they have, and you don't even really know what you want. It's junk, literal junk, stuff other people thought was worthless. That's what makes it great.

In an idealized economy, thrift stores shouldn't exist. Everybody has a living wage, and every product has a durability that exactly matches its desired life; nothing should need to be given away, no one should need to be given to. But then, thrift stores shouldn't work on a customer experience level, either. You wouldn't think an ethos of "let's make everything disorganized and hard to find" would lead to customer satisfaction, but low-budget retailers like TJ Maxx and Ross thrive on this model. People like bargain hunting as much for the hunting as the bargain; it's part of the experience, spending time as if it's a wager. There's a thrill, occasionally, in inefficiency.

In sports, the modern overuse of the word "inefficiency" is a condemnation: It insinuates that there is *an* efficiency, a correct way to be found, and that all other ways are wrong ways. It's prevalent in baseball but hardly contained to it; the lifehack, the Silicon Valley disruption are other examples of productivity creep in our daily lives. Their modern success makes plenty of sense. Maximization of resources, after all, is its own puzzle, and an industry of European board games is founded upon it. It's fun to take a system and optimize it, unravel it like a sudoku puzzle. If there's only one kind of genius, after all, there's no way anyone can fail to appreciate it.

Baseball has been hacking away at these perceived inefficiencies since its inception: platoons, bullpens, farm systems were all installed to extract more out of the tools at hand. But it's been a particular badge of the sabermetric movement, from Ken Phelps and his All-Star Team to Ricardo Rincon and the darlings of *Moneyball*. It's business, but it's also an ethos: the idea that there's treasure among the trash, something we all failed to appreciate until someone brought it to light.

It's the myth that made Sidd Finch so enticing, that fuels so many "best shape" narratives and new pitch promises. We all, athletes and unathletic sportswriters, want to believe that there's genius trapped inside us, and that it's just a matter of puzzling out the combination to unlock it. That our art, our style is the next inefficiency, waiting for our own Billy Beane. It's why we root for underdogs, and why we're excited for the Mike Tauchmans and the Eurubiel Durazos, champions of skin-deep mediocrity.

Except we aren't anymore, really. The days of "Free X" have descended beyond the ring of irony and into obscurity. There are still Xs to be freed, or at least one X, duplicated endlessly: Mike Ford, Luke Voit, Max Muncy. The undervalued one-dimensional slugger demonstrated how the game hasn't quite culturally caught up to its logical extreme. But for those who don't fit the rather spacious mold, times are grimmer. As Rob Arthur revealed several months ago, there's been a marked increase in the number of sub-replacement relievers. It's the outcome of a greater number of teams forced to play out games without the talent to win them, but it's also emblematic of the modern tendency of teams to dispose of their disposable assets, burning through cost-controlled arms the way that man chopped down forests in *The Lorax*. Stuff just isn't built to outlive their original owners anymore.

It's unsurprising, given how well-mined the market for inefficiencies has been of late. The disciples of the early analytics departments, and the disciples of those, have proliferated the league, with only a few backwater holdouts. The league has grown smarter, but every team has learned the same lesson. In fact, the phenomenon creates a peculiar kind of feedback loop: As teams value a specific subset of players or skills, prospective athletes learn to increase their own marketability by conforming themselves to the demands of their prospective employers.

And that's tragic, in the way that the extinction of animals is tragic; a certain amount of biodiversity in baseball has been lost. Shortstops hit like outfielders. Pitchers don't hit at all. Only the catchers remain idiosyncratic, thanks to the defensive demands of their position; eventually they too will be required to produce like everyone else, or they'll meet the fate of their battery mates. A perfect economy requires perfect production.

I mentioned earlier that more and more, I leave thrift stores empty-handed. It is true that I am more discerning than in the past; my bookshelves are full, and there are more streaming films than I will ever be able to watch. But there are other factors at play.

Thrift stores are, in a way, the bond markets of retail. When the economy is rough and other retailers are struggling, more people look secondhand for their products. But as recently as last year, publications were noting a reversal of the trend: Companies like Goodwill and Savers were expanding despite a strong economy. Publications credited a heightened sense of environmentalism and a rejection of cutting-edge fashion as drivers behind the increase, though the more likely answer is the modern American economy hasn't showered its favors equally, particularly among the young.

But it is more than just the economy. Baseball and thrift stores share something else in common, evident in our current conversations about re-starting the sport: They live in the gray area between public service and private enterprise. Thrift stores provide affordable necessities to lower-class citizens, and collectibles and fashion for the middle-class. Because of the success of the latter, prices have gone up across the board. Especially in terms of clothing, the middle-class flight from fashion into vintage has instead carried the aftereffects of fashion, including its costs, into a territory where people just want clothes. But there's another factor in the rise of prices, in the form of the internet.

The Goodwills of the world have grown smarter, too, employing the internet to extract full value from their detritus. Ebay, similarly, has lost much of the charm it had as a new frontier around the turn of the century. Everything has a price point now; even individual taste is no match for the algorithm, because anything rare, no matter how niche its market, is a collectible to someone.

The internet has had the same effect on thrift stores that sabermetrics has had on baseball; its equivalent to OBP was the bar scanner. As detailed in Slate, the rise of second-party stores on eBay and Amazon birthed an entire industry of used-good salespeople, armed with PDAs and scanners, buying books for three dollars to sell online for five. The author, Michael Savitz, reports earning $60,000 by working nearly 80 hours a week; he makes it clear that this is not a vocation of his choosing. It's long hours, with no real creativity or individuality, skimming the cream off of a local establishment and flipping it to someone with a little more money on the other side of the country. And once the vocation exists, the obvious question arises: why wait to put the wares out on the shelves? Why allow value to exist at all?

Nothing is ruined. Thrift stores will continue to sell polo shirts and DVDs, and baseball will continue to exist and make or lose money, depending on who you believe. But as we continue to refine our knowledge, we lose something in the conquest for efficiency, a delight born out of the unknown. The problem isn't the efficiency itself; we can't blame the booksellers, or the people sweeping freeways to collect grams of platinum from damaged catalytic converters. The problem is a system that requires this sort of profit-skimming behavior in order to feed families (or, for corporations, maximize shareholder return).

In times like these, with the 2020 season on the brink and the collective bargaining agreement close behind, it can often feel like the current situation is untenable. It can't keep going like this, even if we don't know what to do about it. But as with thrift stores, there's an equally irresistible feeling that it *has* to keep going, that it would be unimaginable to not have this broken, amazing sport. Both industries exist on an invisible foundation of friction, of chaos and unpredictability, even as both see their foundations buffed down to a perfect, untouchable polish. But if COVID-19 and its financial ramifications do, as some have suggested, make it such that the baseball that returns is fundamentally different than the baseball that came before, perhaps this is the time to lean in, and change the game even more. Fix bunting. Make defense more difficult. Create viable, alternate strategies. Add some chaos back into baseball. It's fun when no one knows quite where things are.

—Patrick Dubuque is an author of Baseball Prospectus.

Steve Dalkowski Dreaming

by Steven Goldman

We dream of being a pitcher, of starring in the major leagues. Depending on your age and your sense of historical perspective, you might imagine yourself as Walter Johnson, throwing harder than anyone else—hitting more batters than anyone else, too, but always feeling bad about it. You could picture yourself as a Tom Seaver or a David Cone, with all the stuff in the world but still being cerebral about it, thinking about so much more than burning 'em in there. There are so many models one could choose: You could be a Lefty Gomez, Jim Bouton, or Bill Lee, skilled, but not taking the whole thing too seriously, or a Lefty Grove, Bob Gibson, or Steve Carlton, powerful but treating each start like a mission to be survived instead of a game to be enjoyed.

Very few would dream of being Steve Dalkowski, the former Baltimore Orioles prospect who died of COVID-19 last week at the age of 80. Yet, there is something just as noble in Dalkowski's negative accomplishments—and accomplishments is what they are—as there is in the precision-engineered pitching of a Greg Maddux. You have to be very good to be that bad. Dalkowski had all of the stuff of the greatest pitchers but none of the command; his story is not one of failing to conquer his limitations, but striving against one of the cruelest hands that fate or genetics or personality can deal us: A desire to achieve great things which is almost but not quite matched by the ability to meet that goal.

As with Johnson, Grove, Bob Feller, and the rest of the hard-throwing pitchers who played before the advent of modern radar guns, we have to take the word of the players and coaches who saw Dalkowski pitch as to his velocity. He was a hard-drinking, maximum-effort pitcher who, if their memories are to be believed, consistently threw over 100 miles per hour. His was the Maltese Fastball, the stuff that dreams are made of. The problem is that velocity without command and control is still a good distance from utility. Dalkowski was the most effective towel you could design for a fish, the sleekest bathing suit intended to be worn by an astronaut, but that doesn't mean he wasn't beautiful: We can appreciate a journey even if it doesn't end at the intended destination.

Whether because of sloppy mechanics he couldn't calm, an inability to understand that a consistent 98 in the strike zone would likely be more effective than a consistent 110 out of it, or all that beer, Dalkowski could never make the adjustments that pitchers like Feller and Nolan Ryan made before him, possibly because he had so far to go: Feller, who never pitched in the minors, came up at 17 and spent three years walking almost seven batters per nine innings before settling in at 3.8 beginning when he was 20. Ryan started out walking over six batters per nine but gradually improved as his long career played out; for him to go from 6.2 walks per nine with the 1966 Greenville Mets to 3.7 with the 1989 Texas Rangers represents a 40 percent reduction. An equivalent improvement by Dalkowski would still have left him walking over 11 batters per nine innings.

Dalkowski was like *The Room* of pitchers, a player so bad he became good again. Cal Ripken, Sr., who both played with and managed Dalkowski, recalled in a 1979 *Sporting News* "where are they now" piece the occasion when the pitcher crossed up his catcher and his fastball, "hit the plate umpire smack in the mask. The mask broke all to pieces and the umpire wound up in the hospital for three days with a concussion. If they ever had a radar gun in those days, I'll bet Dalkowski would have been timed at 110 miles an hour."

Signed by the Orioles out of New Britain High in Connecticut in 1957, Dalkowski was sent to Kingsport in the Appalachian League, where he pitched 62 innings. He allowed only 22 hits in 62 innings, or 3.2 per nine, a number with no equivalent in major league history (though Aroldis Chapman came close in 2014), and also struck out 121 (17.6 per nine) and walked 129 (18.7). He was also charged with 39 wild pitches. That June, one of his fastballs clipped a Dodgers prospect named Bob Beavers and carried away part of his ear. "The first pitch was over the backstop, the second pitch was called a strike, I didn't think it was," Beavers said last year. "The third pitch hit me and knocked me out, so I don't remember much after that. I couldn't get in the sun for a while, and I never did play baseball again." Former minor leaguer Ron Shelton based the *Bull Durham* pitcher Nuke LaLoosh on Dalkowski. And yet, to see him as a figure of fun, an amusing loser, is to misunderstand something unique and strange.

Dalkowski kept on posting some of the strangest lines in baseball history. Pitching for the Stockton Ports of the Class C California League in 1960, he struck out 262 and walked 262 in 170 innings. Yet, he did improve, especially after pitching for Earl Weaver at Elmira in 1962. Weaver had previously had Dalkowski at Aberdeen in 1959, but wasn't ready to grapple with him then. This time he was. "I had grown more and more concerned about players with great physical abilities who could not learn to correct certain basic deficiencies no matter how much you instructed or drilled them," he related in his autobiography, *It's What You Learn After You Know It All That Counts*. He got permission from the Orioles to give all of his players the Stanford-Binet IQ test. "Dalkowski finished in the 1 percentile in his ability to understand facts. Steve, it was said to say, had the ability to do everything but learn." [sic]

IQ tests are problematic diagnostic tools, so take Weaver's estimate of Dalkowski's mental capabilities with a grain of salt. What's important is that even if he got to the right answer by way of the wrong reason, Weaver had learned something valuable. His insight was to stop asking Dalkowski to learn new pitches and just let him get by with the two that he had. Were Dalkowski a prospect today, that would have been a no-brainer: Can't develop a third pitch? The bullpen is right over there, sir. Player development wasn't like that then, but Weaver, temporarily Dalkowski's mentor, could let him work with what he had. According to Weaver, the pitcher responded: "In the final 57 innings he pitched that season Dalkowski gave up 1 earned run, struck out 110 batters, and walked only 11." It's not true—as per the *Elmira Star-Gazette*, as of late July, Dalkowski had walked 71 in 106 innings and finished with 114 in 160 innings, which means Dalkowski's control actually faded at the end of the season rather than improved—but that doesn't mean it didn't happen in some sense, just that it didn't happen that way. Again, it's the journey, not the destination, and his ERA was 3.04 so *something* had gone right.

Also along the way: The next spring, Orioles manager Billy Hitchcock was rooting for Dalkowski to make the team as a long-man—maybe Weaver had gotten through to him. There were things out of Weaver's control, like the universe's twisted sense of humor: that March, Dalkowski's elbow went "twang."

You sometimes read that it was the Orioles' insistence on Dalkowski learning the curve that did him in, but even if they hadn't learned their lesson, the injury was probably just a coincidence: Dalkowski had thrown an incredible number of pitches over the previous few years. Still, it testifies to the dangers of trying to get what you want and risking the loss of what you had. Dalkowski tried to come back, but the 110-mph stuff was gone. A pitcher with no control and no stuff is…a civilian. What followed were years of vagabond living, arrests for drunkenness. There were Alcoholics Anonymous meetings, assistance from baseball alumni associations, but none of it took. From the 1990s until the time of his passing he dwelt in an assisted living facility, suffering from alcohol-related dementia. He'd been a heavy drinker since his teenage years. As with all those pitches per game, there was a price to be paid. You make choices on the journey and some of them are irrevocable. It's like a fairy tale: "Bite of poison apple? Don't mind if I do."

In the aforementioned *Sporting News* profile, Chuck Stevens, the head of the Association of Professional Ballplayers of America, a ballplayer charity, said, "I've got nothing against drinking. I do it myself sometimes. But, I don't condone common drunkenness. We went through lots of heartache and many dollars, but Dalkowski didn't want to help himself and we weren't going to keep him drunk." The journey is *un*like a fairy tale: No one will come along and kiss it better, not if they're busy forming judgments.

In the end, we are left with a sort of philosophical chicken/egg conundrum: Is failing to meet your goals evidence of unfulfilled potential or the lack of it? Isn't what you did by definition what you were capable of doing? Or could you have broken through to something better with the right help, the right lucky break? These are unanswerable questions, and how we try to answer them may say more about us than about the people we're judging.

No pitcher ever has it easy. *All* pitchers must work hard. *All* pitchers must refine their craft. It's almost never just about *stuff*. Dalkowski dreaming is no insult to the great pitchers who made it; from Pete Alexander to Max Scherzer, they have all earned their way up. And yet, if it is true that we can only do as much as we can do, then the journey would be more of an adventure, the ultimate triumph or defeat more noble, if like Dalkowski we lacked 100 percent of the confidence, the command, the self-possession, the commitment, the resistance to making bad decisions that so many great players possess—to be gloriously human. Or, to put it more succinctly, it would be fun to be able to throw as hard as any person ever has. Even if just for a moment, and even if nothing more came of it than that, no one could say you hadn't lived life to the fullest.

—*Steven Goldman is an author of Baseball Prospectus.*

A Reward For A Functioning Society

by Cory Frontin and Craig Goldstein

On July 5, Nationals reliever Sean Doolittle said in the middle of a press conference regarding the restart of Major League Baseball and what would later be known as summer camp, "sports are like the reward of a functioning society." This sentence was amidst a much longer, thoughtful reply about the societal and health conditions under which MLB players were being brought back. It's a very similar sentiment to one Jane McManus used on April 7, when she discussed the White House's meeting with sports commissioners. She said "sports are the effect of a functioning society—not the precursor."

Both versions of the same sentiment spoke to a laudable ideal in the context of a country that was not addressing a rampaging virus, and opting instead to bring sports back for the feeling of normalcy rather than the reality of it. "Priorities," as McManus said.

On Wednesday, the NBA's Milwaukee Bucks conducted a wildcat/political strike, refusing to come out for Game 5 of their playoff series against the Orlando Magic. The Magic refused to accept the forfeit, and shortly thereafter other playoff series were threatened by player strikes. Eventually the league moved to postpone that day's games, folding to players leveraging their united power.

The backdrop against which these actions took place was the shooting by police of Jacob Blake. Blake was shot in the back seven times by police, as he attempted to get into his vehicle. He managed to survive the assault, but is paralyzed from the waist down.

⚾   ⚾   ⚾

The step taken to walk out, first by the Milwaukee Bucks, then subsequently by other NBA, WNBA, and MLB teams, was a step toward upholding the virtue of the sentiment described by McManus and Doolittle. But that sentiment does not align with the broad history of sports in this and other countries, a history that contradicts the core of the idealistic statement.

Sports have been a significant part of American society for most of its existence, expanding in importance and influence in recent years. The idea that society was functioning in a way that was worthy of the reward of sports for most of that time is laughable. Much of America is not functioning and has not functioned for Black people, full stop. The oppressed people at the center of this political act by players, specifically Black players, in concert throughout the NBA and in fits and starts throughout Major League Baseball, have not known a society that functions for them rather than *because* of them.

Politics has been part of the sports landscape since the inception of sport, but for just about as long people have bemoaned its presence. Sports are to be an escape, it is said. An escape from what, though? A functioning society?

No, the presence of sports has never signified a cultural or political system that is on the up and up. Rather, the presence of sports *reflect and reinforce the society that produces them.*

⚾ ⚾ ⚾

The Negro Leagues were born out of societal dysfunction. The need for entirely separate leagues, composed of Black and Latino players barred from the Major Leagues because of racism? That is not a functioning society, and yet there were sports.

Even the integration of players from the Negro Leagues resulted in a transfer of power and wealth from Black-owned businesses and communities and into white ones, mirroring the dysfunction that had bled into every aspect of American society at the time. Japheth Knopp noted in the Spring 2016 Baseball Research Journal:

> *The manner in which integration in baseball—and in American businesses generally—occurred was not the only model which was possible. It was likely not even the best approach available, but rather served the needs of those in already privileged positions who were able to control not only the manner in which desegregation occurred, but the public perception of it as well in order to exploit the situation for financial gain. Indeed, the very word integration may not be the most applicable in this context because what actually transpired was not so much the fair and equitable combination of two subcultures into one equal and more homogenous group, but rather the reluctant allowance—under certain preconditions—for African Americans to be assimilated into white society.*

To understand the value of a movement, though, is not to understand how it is co-opted by ownership, but to know the people it brings together and what they demand. When Jackie Robinson—the player who demarcated the inevitability of the end of the Negro leagues—attended the March on Washington for Jobs and Freedom in 1963, he did so with his family and marched alongside the people. He stood alongside hundreds of thousands to fight for their common civil and labor rights. "The moral arc of the universe is long," many freedom fighters have echoed, "but it bends towards justice." The bend, it is less frequently said, happens when a great mass of people place the moral arc of the universe on their knee and apply force, as Jackie, his family, and thousands of others did that day.

⚾ ⚾ ⚾

Of course, taking the moral arc of the universe down from the mantle and bending it is not without risk. Perhaps the outsized influence of athletes is itself a mark of a dysfunctional society, but, nonetheless, hundreds of athletes woke up on Wednesday morning with the power to bring in millions of dollars in revenues. That very power, as we would come to find out, was matched with the equal and opposite power to *not* bring those revenues. That power, in hands ranging from the Milwaukee Bucks, to Kenny Smith in the *Inside the NBA* Studio, from the unexpected ally, Josh Hader, and his largely white teammates to the notably Black Seattle Mariners, would be exercised for a single demand: the end to state violence against Black people. Not unlike the March itself, it sat at the intersection of the civil rights of Black Americans and bold labor action. The March on Washington stood in the face of a false notion of integration—against an integration of extraction but not one of equality—and proposed something different. Just the same, the acts of solidarity of August 26, 2020 will be remembered in stark defiance of MLB's BLM-branded, but ultimately empty displays on opening weekend.

Bold defiance like this can never be without risk. By choosing to exercise this power, the Milwaukee Bucks took a risk. They risked vitriol and backlash from those they disagreed with. They risked fines or seeing their contracts voided, as a walkout like this is prohibited by their CBA. They risked forfeiting a playoff game, one that, as the No. 1 seed in the playoffs, they'd worked all year to attain. They didn't know how Orlando would respond. It wasn't clear that other teams throughout the league would follow suit in solidarity. And it wasn't known the league would accept these actions and moderately co-opt them by "postponing" games that would have featured no players.

If the league reschedules the games, some of the athletes' risk—their shared sacrifice—will be diminished, in retrospect. But they did not know any of that when they took that risk. And it is often left to athletes to take these risks when others in society won't, especially those of their same socioeconomic status and levels of influence.

It is athletes, specifically BIPOC athletes, that take them, though, because they live with the risk of being something other than white in this country every day. They are no strangers to the realities of police brutality. It seems incongruous then, to say that sports are a reward for a functioning society when we rely on athletes to lead us closer to being a functioning society. Luckily, our beloved athletes, WNBA players first and foremost among them, understand what sports truly are: a pipebender for the moral arc of the universe.

—Craig Goldstein is editor in chief of Baseball Prospectus. Cory Frontin is an author of Baseball Prospectus.

Index of Names

Anderson, Brett 44
Arcia, Orlando 16
Ashby, Aaron 85, 92
Austin, Tyler 74
Bettinger, Alec 86
Braun, Ryan 18
Burnes, Corbin 46
Cain, Lorenzo 75
Feliciano, Mario 76, 94
Feyereisen, J.P. 48
File, Dylan 86
Fisher, Derek 77
García, Avisaíl 20
Garcia, Eduardo 78, 98
Gyorko, Jedd 22
Hader, Josh 50
Henry, Payton 78
Hiura, Keston 24
Houser, Adrian 52
Hummel, Cooper 79
Kelly, Antoine 87, 95
Lauer, Eric 54
Lazar, Max 87
Lindblom, Josh 56
Lopes, Tim 26
Lutz, Tristen 79, 94
Maile, Luke 80
Mathias, Mark 28
Milner, Hoby 58
Mitchell, Garrett 80, 92
Narváez, Omar 30
Nottingham, Jacob 32
Peralta, Freddy 60
Perdomo, Angel 88
Perez, Hedbert 81, 97
Peterson, Jace 81
Piña, Manny 34
Rasmussen, Drew 62
Ray, Corey 81
Rodriguez, Carlos 96
Small, Ethan 89, 93
Sogard, Eric 82
Suter, Brent 64
Taylor, Tyrone 36
Topa, Justin 66
Turang, Brice 83, 91
Urías, Luis 38
Vogelbach, Daniel 84
Warren, Zavier 98
Williams, Devin 68
Wong, Kolten 40
Woodruff, Brandon 70
Yardley, Eric 72
Yelich, Christian 42
Zamora, Freddy 85, 96

For the Joy of Keeping Score

THIRTY81 Project is an ongoing graphic design project focused on the ballparks of baseball. Since being established in 2013, scorecards have been a fundamental part of the effort. Each two-page card is uniquely ballpark-centric — there are 30 variants — and designed with both beginning and veteran scorekeepers in mind. Evolving over the years with suggestions from fans, broadcasters, and official scorers, the sheets are freely available to everyone as printable letter-size PDFs at the project webshop: www.THIRTY81Project.com

Download, Print, Score, Repeat ...

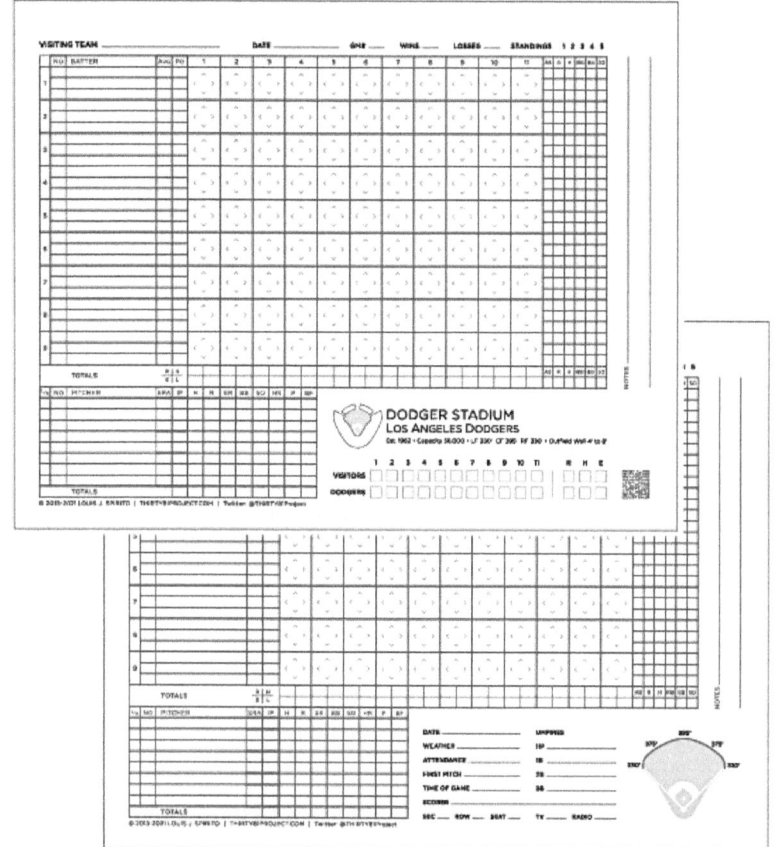

Scorecard design ©2013-2021 Louis J. Spirito | THIRTY81Project